Right to Private Property

Other Books in the Issues on Trial Series:

Contents

Chapter 1: If Land Loses All Value Due to Restrictions, the Government Must Pay

Chapter 2: The Government Need Not Pay for Land if Its Use Is Temporarily Restricted

Chapter 3: Cities May Condemn Homes to Make Way for Commercial Development

Chapter 4: Landowners Cannot Sue the Government for Harassing Them over Land

Foreword

The U.S. courts have long served as a battleground for the most highly charged and contentious issues of the time. Divisive matters are often brought into the legal system by activists who feel strongly for their cause and demand an official resolution. Indeed, subjects that give rise to intense emotions or involve closely held religious or moral beliefs lay at the heart of the most polemical court rulings in history. One such case was *Brown v. Board of Education* (1954), which ended racial segregation in schools. Prior to *Brown*, the courts had held that blacks could be forced to use separate facilities as long as these facilities were equal to that of whites.

For years many groups had opposed segregation based on religious, moral, and legal grounds. Educators produced heartfelt testimony that segregated schooling greatly disadvantaged black children. They noted that in comparison to whites, blacks received a substandard education in deplorable conditions. Religious leaders such as Martin Luther King Jr. preached that the harsh treatment of blacks was immoral and unjust. Many involved in civil rights law, such as Thurgood Marshall, called for equal protection of all people under the law, as their study of the Constitution had indicated that segregation was illegal and un-American. Whatever their motivation for ending the practice, and despite the threats they received from segregationists, these ardent activists remained unwavering in their cause.

Those fighting against the integration of schools were mainly white southerners who did not believe that whites and blacks should intermingle. Blacks were subordinate to whites, they maintained, and society had to resist any attempt to break down strict color lines. Some white southerners charged that segregated schooling was *not* hindering blacks' education. For example, Virginia attorney general J. Lindsay Almond as-

serted, "With the help and the sympathy and the love and respect of the white people of the South, the colored man has
risen under that educational process to a place of eminence
and respect throughout the nation. It has served him well." So
when the Supreme Court ruled against the segregationists in
Brown, the South responded with vociferous cries of protest.
Even government leaders criticized the decision. The governor
of Arkansas, Orval Faubus, stated that he would not "be a
party to any attempt to force acceptance of change to which
the people are so overwhelmingly opposed." Indeed, resistance
to integration was so great that when black students arrived at
the formerly all-white Central High School in Arkansas, federal troops had to be dispatched to quell a threatening mob of
protesters.

Nevertheless, the *Brown* decision was enforced and the
South integrated its schools. In this instance, the Court, while
not settling the issue to everyone's satisfaction, functioned as
an instrument of progress by forcing a major social change.
Historian David Halberstam observes that the *Brown* ruling
"deprived segregationist practices of their moral legitimacy. . . .
It was therefore perhaps the single most important moment
of the decade, the moment that separated the old order from
the new and helped create the tumultuous era just arriving."
Considered one of the most important victories for civil rights,
Brown paved the way for challenges to racial segregation in
many areas, including on public buses and in restaurants.

In examining *Brown*, it becomes apparent that the courts
play an influential role—and face an arduous challenge—in
shaping the debate over emotionally charged social issues.
Judges must balance competing interests, keeping in mind the
high stakes and intense emotions on both sides. As exempli-
fied by *Brown*, judicial decisions often upset the status quo
and initiate significant changes in society. Greenhaven Press's
Issues on Trial series captures the controversy surrounding influential court rulings and explores the social ramifications of

such decisions from varying perspectives. Each anthology highlights one social issue—such as the death penalty, students' rights, or wartime civil liberties. Each volume then focuses on key historical and contemporary court cases that helped mold the issue as we know it today. The books include a compendium of primary sources—court rulings, dissents, and immediate reactions to the rulings—as well as secondary sources from experts in the field, people involved in the cases, legal analysts, and other commentators opining on the implications and legacy of the chosen cases. An annotated table of contents, an in-depth introduction, and prefaces that overview each case all provide context as readers delve into the topic at hand. To help students fully probe the subject, each volume contains book and periodical bibliographies, a comprehensive index, and a list of organizations to contact. With these features, the Issues on Trial series offers a well-rounded perspective on the courts' role in framing society's thorniest, most impassioned debates.

Introduction

Owning land has always been important to Americans. In recent times, home ownership has been the pride of middle-class families and the goal, or at least the dream, of those less fortunate. The desire to own land has been a prime factor in the settlement of America since the time of the earliest colonists; it was one of the things that brought them here in the first place. In Europe, land was scarce and was available only to the wealthy upper class; there were limits on who could acquire it and what rights in it they could possess. In the New World, a seemingly infinite supply was free for the taking. As eminent historian Edmund Morgan wrote in *The Birth of the Republic,* "The widespread ownership of property is perhaps the most important single fact about Americans of the Revolutionary period.... Standing on his own land with spade in hand and flintlock not far off, the American could look at his richest neighbor and laugh."

As the population grew, the hunger to own land drove settlers westward. Anyone willing to work hard could gain possession not merely of a home, but of a whole farm. The government encouraged this with the Homestead Act of 1862, which gave 160 acres outside the original thirteen colonies to whoever built on it, land that could be kept and passed on to children or else sold at a profit. In this way ordinary people achieved prosperity and independence. "Land ownership is not a sideshow to the American experience," says Carla T. Main in the journal *Policy Review.* "It is a central component of what makes us American."

Although plenty of free land existed in early America, the founders of the nation realized that the government would have to acquire some privately owned property for community use, and they remembered all too well that in England the sovereign could seize a subject's land at will. Thus, when the Bill of Rights was added to the Constitution, a provision known as the takings clause was included in the Fifth Amendment to ensure that people would not be unfairly deprived of their property. Among other things the federal government cannot do, it states: ". . . nor shall private property be taken for public use without just compensation." In other words, if the government takes someone's land, it has to pay for it. In most cases, landowners were not hurt by such takings, since they could easily move to new locations. Moreover, the government already owned most of the land outside settled areas; land controversies concerned its grants to the railroads and to other industries deemed of importance to the nation more than its dealings with individuals.

In the nineteenth century, few people stopped to think that someday the land would run out or that a pressing need to protect wildlife might exist, although the farsightedness of a minority did lead to some conservation efforts and the creation of the first national parks. The idea of the whole country being filled up was simply incomprehensible to the average citizen. Even in the early twentieth century, environmental issues were not of widespread concern. As the century progressed, however, it became more and more apparent that a conflict existed between the traditional right of individuals to own property and a new perception of public responsibility for land use. This conflict has led to bitter controversies to which there are not easy resolutions. Many people believe that constitutionally guaranteed property rights are being unjustifiably violated by government planning and that they must be restored. Others are convinced that government planning of land use is vital both to the economic well-being of the nation and to the preservation of the environment. It is unlikely that these opposing positions can ever be reconciled in a general way; the courts can merely balance the factors in individual cases.

Court disputes often center on the meaning of "public use," which is the only purpose for which the Constitution allows land to be taken against its owner's will. Does it mean actual use for a public facility such as a school or a road, or does any use that benefits the public qualify? The Constitution does not specify. A number of important cases of this type have involved urban renewal. The first of these was *Berman v. Parker* (1954), a case in which the owner of a Washington, D.C., department store resisted the taking of his property because it was in good repair; only others surrounding it—many of which lacked indoor plumbing—were in such poor condition that they endangered public health. He maintained that it would not be "public use" to tear down a perfectly good building. The Supreme Court, however, ruled that the redevelopment plan for an area must be considered as a whole, since removal of all buildings within that area is necessary to its completion. In the majority opinion, Justice William O. Douglas went further; he wrote, "It is within the power of the legislature to determine that the community should be beautiful as well as healthy, spacious as well as clean, well balanced as well as carefully patrolled. . . . If those who govern the District of Columbia decide that the Nation's Capital should be beautiful as well as sanitary, there is nothing in the Fifth Amendment that stands in the way."

This landmark case was a turning point. Before long, urban planners began to look beyond public health considerations. Many "blighted areas" of other cities were destroyed, usually with a disproportionate effect on blacks. In 1981, the city of Detroit bulldozed the entire neighborhood of Poletown, Michigan, to make room for a Cadillac assembly plant. Poletown was occupied by working-class people, mostly of Polish descent, whose homes were not in bad shape. They sued the city, but in a decision commonly viewed as infamous, the Michigan Supreme Court ruled against them. To the relief of property rights advocates it overturned that decision more than twenty years later, long after the homes were gone; because this was a state court decision, however, it did not affect other states. In *Kelo et al. v. City of New London et al.* the U.S. Supreme Court ruled that economic development—the replacement of condemned homes not by better housing but by privately-owned commercial facilities that promise jobs—can indeed be considered public use.

Attorney Carla T. Main argues that contrary to the assertions of some people, the seizure of homes and businesses for economic development purposes is not due merely to greed. In her opinion, it stems from Americans' long-standing relationship with land. "While the urge to build and revitalize was a positive thing for the country so long as the land held out," she writes, "the American lust for land has outlived the days of limitless supply—and that is a dangerous state of affairs for private property owners. What we are now witnessing is the American inability to pass up an opportunity to build or to stand by while things decay . . . running smack up against the end of limitless supply. This has led us to what would have been unthinkable at Jamestown in 1607: We are cannibalizing each other's land in our zeal to keep on building America."

But this is only one aspect of the controversy surrounding land use. The other is the belief of environmentalists that land outside cities should remain in its natural state, and that owners of such land should be restricted in their use of it in order to preserve it for future generations. So between these two factions—the economic development advocates and the opponents of all development—both city and rural homeowners are threatened. Since the *Kelo* decision, a movement to restrict the ability of government to take property has been gaining momentum. It remains to be seen which view of the public good will prevail.

CHAPTER 1

If Land Loses All Value Due to Restrictions, the Government Must Pay

Case Overview

Lucas v. South Carolina Coastal Council (1992)

In 1986 David Lucas, a real estate developer, bought two oceanfront lots on the Isle of Palms, an island off the South Carolina coast. He planned to build a home for himself on one of them and another home, to sell, on the other. But while he was in the process of obtaining a building permit, a new state law—the Beachfront Management Act—was passed as an environmental measure intended to protect the beach. Under this law, constructing buildings within a "critical" distance from the shoreline was forbidden. Although Lucas's lots had been legal to build homes on at the time he purchased them, the rules had changed. He was not allowed to build, and so the lots were worthless to him—even a liability, as he still had to pay property taxes.

Lucas took his case to court, maintaining that because the government had deprived him of the use of his property under the Fifth Amendment to the Constitution it was obliged to pay him for it. This amendment says, among other things, that "private property [shall not] be taken for public use without just compensation," a statement that is known as the "takings clause." It has always been clear that the government must pay for land if it takes physical possession of it, for example, to build a school or a road. However, if it merely regulates the use of the land, the issue is less straightforward. The establishment of such restrictions is called a "regulatory taking," and until 1922 regulatory takings were not considered compensable. In that year, the Supreme Court said that if government restrictions went "too far," the landowner must be paid. "Too far" is, of course, a subjective judgment. During the twentieth century, government regulation of land use became more and more common, so the question of how far it can go before payment is required began to arise.

The trial court agreed with Lucas that his land had become valueless and ordered the government to pay him over $1.2 million. This judgment was appealed to the State Supreme Court, which ruled that new construction in the coastal zone would threaten a public resource and that therefore the ban on it was designed to prevent "harmful or noxious" use of property. Such uses, it said, are similar to public nuisances, and governments can regulate nuisances without paying anything under the takings clause. The lower court's ruling was reversed. When Lucas appealed this decision, the U.S. Supreme Court agreed to review the case.

The Supreme Court majority was not convinced by the argument of the South Carolina court. The distinction between preventing harm and conferring benefits is not firm, it said, and, therefore, harm prevention cannot be the basis for departing from the constitutional requirement that takings must be compensated. It ruled that when government regulations deny a property owner "all economically viable use" of his land, that must be treated as a taking, unless the regulations deal merely with ways in which the landowner had no right to use the property at the time it was acquired. To avoid paying, South Carolina would have to do more than claim that building homes on Lucas's land would not be in the public interest. It would have to prove that doing so would violate some preexisting common law principle concerning nuisances.

The case was sent back to the South Carolina court for this to be determined, and after lengthy complications during which building permits were issued for other nearby lots and Lucas threatened to sue for discrimination, payment was finally agreed upon. This was not the end of the story, however. After the state had to pay for the lots, it soon decided to recoup the cost by selling them—and the new owners were given permission to build.

"[The state] issued a statement even I couldn't believe," Lucas wrote in his book *Lucas vs. the Green Machine*. "They said, in part, that since there are houses on either side of the lots and houses all around, it doesn't make sense to keep the two lots as a park. Instead, the best use for the property is for building single family residences."

Despite this ironic outcome, David Lucas felt that his court battle had achieved much more than merely granting him the money to which he was entitled. He believed that preserving property rights matters to everyone because adhering to the Constitution matters. "Perhaps the most important thing to come out of all this is hope for the future," he wrote. "I have been amazed at the number of people who have fallen prey to the old saw 'You can't fight city hall.' Well, you can. I did and I won. . . . The rights of average Americans still matter."

> "A law or decree [that does not require compensation for property loss] must ... do no more than duplicate the result that could have been achieved in the courts—by adjacent landowners (or other uniquely affected persons) under the State's law of private nuisance."

The Court's Decision: The Government Must Pay Owners for Property Made Worthless by Land-Use Regulations

Antonin Scalia

Antonin Scalia became a justice of the U.S Supreme Court in 1986 and, as of 2008, he is its second most senior member. He is a strong conservative who believes in a strict interpretation of the Constitution, according to the meaning it had when originally adopted. The following is his majority opinion in Lucas v. South Carolina Coastal Council, *in which the Court ruled that David Lucas must be paid for his land after the government ruled that he could not build on it, in an effort to protect the beach. Justice Scalia says that because Lucas lost all economically beneficial uses of his land, he suffered a "taking" to which the takings clause of the Fifth Amendment applied. Although the state claimed that building would be harmful to the environment and Lucas did not dispute their right to ban it, the question of whether they had to pay for the land did not depend on a mere declaration that a prospective use would not be in the*

Antonin Scalia, majority opinion, *Lucas v. South Carolina Coastal Council*, U.S. Supreme Court, June 29, 1992.

public interest. To avoid paying, they would have to prove that such use would violate the common law principle that one cannot use one's property in a way that harms others, just as a neighboring property owner would.

We have ... described at least two discrete categories of regulatory action as compensable without case-specific inquiry into the public interest advanced in support of the restraint. The first encompasses regulations that compel the property owner to suffer a physical "invasion" of his property. In general (at least with regard to permanent invasions), no matter how minute the intrusion, and no matter how weighty the public purpose behind it, we have required compensation. For example, in *Loretto v. Teleprompter Manhattan CATV Corp.*, we determined that New York's law requiring landlords to allow television cable companies to emplace cable facilities in their apartment buildings constituted a taking, even though the facilities occupied, at most, only 1 1/2 cubic feet of the landlords' property.

The second situation in which we have found categorical treatment appropriate is where regulation denies all economically beneficial or productive use of land. As we have said on numerous occasions, the Fifth Amendment is violated when land use regulation "does not substantially advance legitimate state interests or denies an owner economically viable use of his land."

We have never set forth the justification for this rule. Perhaps it is simply, as Justice [William J.] Brennan suggested, that total deprivation of beneficial use is, from the landowner's point of view, the equivalent of a physical appropriation. Surely, at least, in the extraordinary circumstance when no productive or economically beneficial use of land is permitted, it is less realistic to indulge our usual assumption that the legislature is simply "adjusting the benefits and burdens of economic life," [*Penn Central Transportation Co. v. New York City* (1978)], in a manner that secures an "average reciprocity of advantage" to everyone concerned [*Pennsylvania Coal Co. v.*

Mahon (1922)]. And the functional basis for permitting the government, by regulation, to affect property values without compensation—that Government hardly could go on if, to some extent, values incident to property could not be diminished without paying for every such change in the general law—does not apply to the relatively rare situations where the government has deprived a landowner of all economically beneficial uses.

On the other side of the balance, affirmatively supporting a compensation requirement, is the fact that regulations that leave the owner of land without economically beneficial or productive options for its use—typically, as here, by requiring land to be left substantially in its natural state—carry with them a heightened risk that private property is being pressed into some form of public service under the guise of mitigating serious public harm. As Justice Brennan explained: From the government's point of view, the benefits flowing to the public from preservation of open space through regulation may be equally great as from creating a wildlife refuge through formal condemnation or increasing electricity production through a dam project that floods private property. The many statutes on the books, both state and federal, that provide for the use of eminent domain to impose servitudes on private scenic lands preventing developmental uses, or to acquire such lands altogether, suggest the practical equivalence in this setting of negative regulation and appropriation.

We think, in short, that there are good reasons for our frequently expressed belief that, when the owner of real property has been called upon to sacrifice all economically beneficial uses in the name of the common good, that is, to leave his property economically idle, he has suffered a taking.

Building Homes Is Not a Noxious Use of Land

The trial court found [David H.] Lucas' two beachfront lots [on the isle of Palms in Charleston County, South Carolina] to have been rendered valueless by respondent's enforcement of the coastal-zone construction ban. Under Lucas' theory of the case, which rested upon our "no economically viable use" statements, that finding entitled him to compensation. Lucas believed it unnecessary to take issue with either the purposes behind the Beachfront Management Act or the means chosen by the South Carolina Legislature to effectuate those purposes. The South Carolina Supreme Court, however, thought otherwise. In its view, the Beachfront Management Act was no ordinary enactment, but involved an exercise of South Carolina's "police powers" to mitigate the harm to the public interest that petitioner's use of his land might occasion. By neglecting to dispute the findings enumerated in the Act or otherwise to challenge the legislature's purposes, petitioner concede[d] that the beach/dune area of South Carolina's shores is an extremely valuable public resource; that the erection of new construction, inter alia [among other things] contributes to the erosion and destruction of this public resource; and that discouraging new construction in close proximity to the beach/dune area is necessary to prevent a great public harm. In the court's view, these concessions brought petitioner's challenge within a long line of this Court's cases sustaining against Due Process and Takings Clause challenges the State's use of its "police powers" to enjoin a property owner from activities akin to public nuisances.

It is correct that many of our prior opinions have suggested that "harmful or noxious uses" of property may be proscribed by government regulation without the requirement of compensation. For a number of reasons, however, we think the South Carolina Supreme Court was too quick to conclude that that principle decides the present case. The "harmful or noxious uses" principle was the Court's early attempt to describe in theoretical terms why government may, consistent with the Takings Clause, affect property values by regulation without incurring an obligation to compensate—a reality we nowadays acknowledge explicitly with respect to the full scope of the State's police power. . . .

The transition from our early focus on control of "noxious" uses to our contemporary understanding of the broad realm within which government may regulate without compensation was an easy one, since the distinction between "harm-preventing" and "benefit-conferring" regulation is often in the eye of the beholder. It is quite possible, for example, to describe in either fashion the ecological, economic, and esthetic concerns that inspired the South Carolina Legislature in the present case. One could say that imposing a servitude on Lucas' land is necessary in order to prevent his use of it from "harming" South Carolina's ecological resources; or, instead, in order to achieve the "benefits" of an ecological preserve. Whether one or the other of the competing characterizations will come to one's lips in a particular case depends primarily upon one's evaluation of the worth of competing uses of real estate. A given restraint will be seen as mitigating "harm" to the adjacent parcels or securing a "benefit" for them, depending upon he observer's evaluation of the relative importance of the use that the restraint favors. Whether Lucas' construction of single-family residences on his parcels should be described as bringing "harm" to South Carolina's adjacent ecological resources thus depends principally upon whether the describer believes that the State's use interest in nurturing those resources is so important that any competing adjacent use must yield.

When it is understood that "prevention of harmful use" was merely our early formulation of the police power justification necessary to sustain (without compensation) any regulatory diminution in value; and that the distinction between regulation that "prevents harmful use" and that which "confers benefits" is difficult, if not impossible, to discern on an objective, value-free basis; it becomes self-evident that noxious-use logic cannot serve as a touchstone to distinguish regulatory "takings"—which require compensation—from regulatory deprivations that do not require compensation. A fortiori [even more certainly], the legislature's recitation of a noxious-use justification cannot be the basis for departing from our categorical rule that total regulatory takings must be compensated. If it were, departure would virtually always be allowed. The South Carolina Supreme Court's approach would essentially nullify . . . limits to the non-compensable exercise of the police power. Our cases provide no support for this: none of them that employed the logic of "harmful use" prevention to sustain a regulation involved an allegation that the regulation wholly eliminated the value of the claimant's land.

Payment for Land Can Be Avoided Only if It Is Used in Ways Not Originally Allowed

Where the State seeks to sustain regulation that deprives land of all economically beneficial use, we think it may resist compensation only if the logically antecedent inquiry into the nature of the owner's estate shows that the proscribed use interests were not part of his title to begin with. This accords, we think, with our "takings" jurisprudence, which has traditionally been guided by the understandings of our citizens regarding the content of, and the State's power over, the "bundle of rights" that they acquire when they obtain title to property. It seems to us that the property owner necessarily expects the uses of his property to be restricted, from time to time, by various measures newly enacted by the State in legitimate exercise of its police powers; "[a]s long recognized, some values are enjoyed under an implied limitation, and must yield to the police power" [*Pennsylvania Coal Co. v. Mahon*]. And in the case of personal property, by reason of the State's traditionally high degree of control over commercial dealings, he ought to be aware of the possibility that new regulation might even render his property economically worthless (at least if the property's only economically productive use is sale or manufacture for sale). In the case of land, however, we think the notion pressed by the Council that title is somehow held subject to the "implied limitation" that the State may subsequently eliminate all economically valuable use is inconsistent with the historical compact recorded in the Takings Clause that has become part of our constitutional culture.

Where "permanent physical occupation" of land is concerned, we have refused to allow the government to decree it anew (without compensation), no matter how weighty the asserted "public interests" involved—though we assuredly would permit the government to assert a permanent easement that was a pre-existing limitation upon the landowner's title. We believe similar treatment must be accorded confiscatory regulations, i.e., regulations that prohibit all economically beneficial use of land: Any limitation so severe cannot be newly legislated or decreed (without compensation), but must inhere in the title itself, in the restrictions that background principles of the State's law of property and nuisance already place upon land ownership. A law or decree with such an effect must, in other words, do no more than duplicate the result that could have been achieved in the courts—by adjacent landowners (or other uniquely affected persons) under the State's law of private nuisance, or by the State under its complementary power to abate nuisances that affect the public generally, or otherwise.

On this analysis, the owner of a lakebed, for example, would not be entitled to compensation when he is denied the requisite permit to engage in a landfilling operation that would have the effect of flooding others' land. Nor the corporate owner of a nuclear generating plant, when it is directed to remove all improvements from its land upon discovery that the plant sits astride an earthquake fault. Such regulatory action may well have the effect of eliminating the land's only economically productive use, but it does not proscribe a productive use that was previously permissible under relevant property and nuisance principles. The use of these properties for what are now expressly prohibited purposes was always unlawful, and (subject to other constitutional limitations) it was open to the State at any point to make the implication of those background principles of nuisance and property law explicit. In light of our traditional resort to "existing rules or understandings that stem from an independent source such as state law" to define the range of interests that qualify for protection as "property" under the Fifth and Fourteenth Amendments, this recognition that the Takings Clause does not require compensation when an owner is barred from putting land to a use that is proscribed by those "existing rules or understandings" is surely unexceptional. When, however, a regulation that declares "off limits" all economically productive or beneficial uses of land goes beyond what the relevant background principles would dictate, compensation must be paid to sustain it.

The "total taking" inquiry we require today will ordinarily entail (as the application of state nuisance law ordinarily entails) analysis of, among other things, the degree of harm to public lands and resources, or adjacent private property, posed by the claimant's proposed activities, and the relative ease with which the alleged harm can be avoided through measures taken by the claimant and the government (or adjacent private landowners) alike. The fact that a particular use has long been engaged in by similarly situated owners ordinarily imports a lack of any common law prohibition (though changed circumstances or new knowledge may make what was previously permissible no longer so). So also does the fact that other landowners, similarly situated, are permitted to continue the use denied to the claimant.

It seems unlikely that common law principles would have prevented the erection of any habitable or productive improvements on petitioner's land; they rarely support prohibition of the "essential use" of land. The question, however, is one of state law to be dealt with on remand. We emphasize that, to win its case, South Carolina must do more than proffer the legislature's declaration that the uses Lucas desires are inconsistent with the public interest, or the conclusory assertion that they violate a common law maxim such as sic utere tuo ut alienum non laedas [you cannot use your property in a way harmful to others]. As we have said, a "State, by ipse dixit [an unproven statement] may not transform private property into public property without compensation . . ." [*Webb's Fabulous Pharmacies, Inc. v. Beckwith* (1980)]. Instead, as it would be required to do if it sought to restrain Lucas in a common law action for public nuisance, South Carolina must identify background principles of nuisance and property law that prohibit the uses he now intends in the circumstances in which the property is presently found. Only on this showing can the State fairly claim that, in proscribing all such beneficial uses, the Beachfront Management Act is taking nothing.

> "Long ago it was recognized that all property in this country is held under the implied obligation that the owner's use of it shall not be injurious to the community."

Dissenting Opinion: The Constitution Does Not Require Payment for Land Made Worthless by Government Regulations

Harry Blackmun

Harry Blackmun was a justice of the Supreme Court from 1970 to 1994. He is best known as the author of the majority opinion in Roe v. Wade, *the decision that overturned laws restricting abortion. The following is his dissenting opinion in* Lucas v. South Carolina Coastal Council, *in which he strongly criticizes the Court's decision. He argues that building on the lots owned by Lucas would have been harmful, that Lucas did not contest this, and that under precedents previously established by the Court, the building ban should not be considered a taking and therefore should not require any compensation for Lucas's loss. Furthermore, Justice Blackmun contests the Court's establishment of a new rule for evaluating regulations that will also apply to other cases where they cause land to lose all its value. There is no basis in history, he says, for the principle that restrictions on property use are takings unless the use they prohibit is a com-*

Harry Blackmun, dissenting opinion, *Lucas v. South Carolina Coastal Council*, U.S. Supreme Court, June 29, 1992.

mon law nuisance that harms neighbors. Past decisions have de-pended on whether the benefit to the public was sufficient to prohibit the use in spite of the cost to the landowner.

Today the Court launches a missile to kill a mouse.

The State of South Carolina prohibited petitioner [David] Lucas from building a permanent structure on his property from 1988 to 1990. Relying on an unreviewed (and implausible) state trial court finding that this restriction left Lucas' property valueless, this Court granted review to deter-mine whether compensation must be paid in cases where the State prohibits all economic use of real estate. According to the Court, such an occasion never has arisen in any of our prior cases, and the Court imagines that it will arise "relatively rarely" or only in "extraordinary circumstances." Almost cer-tainly, it did not happen in this case.

Nonetheless, the Court presses on to decide the issue, and as it does, it ignores its jurisdictional limits, remakes its tradi-tional rules of review, and creates simultaneously a new cat-egorical rule and an exception (neither of which is rooted in our prior case law, common law, or common sense). I protest not only the Court's decision, but each step taken to reach it. More fundamentally, I question the Court's wisdom in issuing sweeping new rules to decide such a narrow case. Surely, . . . the Court could have reached the result it wanted without in-flicting this damage upon our Takings Clause jurisprudence.

My fear is that the Court's new policies will spread beyond the narrow confines of the present case. For that reason, I, like the Court, will give far greater attention to this case than its narrow scope suggests—not because I can intercept the Court's missile, or save the targeted mouse, but because I hope per-haps to limit the collateral damage. . . .

If the Building Ban Prevents Harm, It Is Constitutional

The South Carolina Supreme Court found that the Beachfront Management Act did not take petitioner's property without compensation. The decision rested on two premises that, until today, were unassailable—that the State has the power to prevent any use of property it finds to be harmful to its citizens, and that a state statute is entitled to a presumption of constitutionality.

The Beachfront Management Act includes a finding by the South Carolina General Assembly that the beach/dune system serves the purpose of "protect[ing] life and property by serving as a storm barrier which dissipates wave energy and contributes to shoreline stability in an economical and effective manner."

If the state legislature is correct that the prohibition on building in front of the setback line prevents serious harm, then, under this Court's prior cases, the Act is constitutional. Long ago it was recognized that all property in this country is held under the implied obligation that the owner's use of it shall not be injurious to the community, and the Takings Clause did not transform that principle to one that requires compensation whenever the State asserts its power to enforce it. The Court consistently has upheld regulations imposed to arrest a significant threat to the common welfare, whatever their economic effect on the owner.

Petitioner never challenged the legislature's findings that a building ban was necessary to protect property and life. Nor did he contend that the threatened harm was not sufficiently serious to make building a house in a particular location a "harmful" use, that the legislature had not made sufficient findings, or that the legislature was motivated by anything other than a desire to minimize damage to coastal areas. Indeed, petitioner objected at trial that evidence as to the purposes of the setback requirement was irrelevant. The South

Carolina Supreme Court accordingly understood petitioner not to contest the State's position that "discouraging new construction in close proximity to the beach/dune area is necessary to prevent a great public harm," and "to prevent serious injury to the community." The court considered itself "bound by these uncontested legislative findings . . . [in the absence of] any attack whatsoever on the statutory scheme."

Nothing in the record undermines the General Assembly's assessment that prohibitions on building in front of the setback line are necessary to protect people and property from storms, high tides, and beach erosion. Because that legislative determination cannot be disregarded in the absence of such evidence, and because its determination of harm to life and property from building is sufficient to prohibit that use under this Court's cases, the South Carolina Supreme Court correctly found no taking. . . .

The Court creates its new taking jurisprudence based on the trial court's finding that the property had lost all economic value. This finding is almost certainly erroneous. Petitioner still can enjoy other attributes of ownership, such as the right to exclude others, "one of the most essential sticks in the bundle of rights that are commonly characterized as property" [*Kaiser Aetna v. United States* (1979)]. Petitioner can picnic, swim, camp in a tent, or live on the property in a movable trailer. State courts frequently have reorganized that land has economic value where the only residual economic uses are recreation or camping. . . .

The Court Has Ignored Precedents and Altered Rules of Review

The Court's willingness to dispense with precedent in its haste to reach a result is not limited to its initial jurisdictional decision. The Court also alters the long-settled rules of review.

The South Carolina Supreme Court's decision to defer to legislative judgments in the absence of a challenge from petitioner comports with one of this Court's oldest maxims: "The existence of facts supporting the legislative judgment is to be presumed" [*United States v. Carolene Products Co.* (1938)].

Accordingly, this Court always has required plaintiffs challenging the constitutionality of an ordinance to provide "some factual foundation of record" that contravenes the legislative findings.... In the absence of such proof, "the presumption of constitutionality must prevail."

Rather than invoking these traditional rules, the Court decides the State has the burden to convince the courts that its legislative judgments are correct. Despite Lucas' complete failure to contest the legislature's findings of serious harm to life and property if a permanent structure is built, the Court decides that the legislative findings are not sufficient to justify the use prohibition. Instead, the Court "emphasize[s]" the State must do more than merely proffer its legislative judgments to avoid invalidating its law. In this case, apparently, the State now has the burden of showing the regulation is not a taking. The Court offers no justification for its sudden hostility toward state legislators, and I doubt that it could.

The Court does not reject the South Carolina Supreme Court's decision simply on the basis of its disbelief and distrust of the legislature's findings. It also takes the opportunity to create a new scheme for regulations that eliminate all economic value. From now on, there is a categorical rule finding these regulations to be a taking unless the use they prohibit is a background common law nuisance or property principle.

I first question the Court's rationale in creating a category that obviates a "case-specific inquiry into the public interest advanced," if all economic value has been lost. If one fact about the Court's takings jurisprudence can be stated without contradiction, it is that "the particular circumstances of each case" determine whether a specific restriction will be rendered invalid by the government's failure to pay compensation [*United States v. Central Eureka Mining Co.* (1958)]. This is so because, although we have articulated certain factors to be considered, including the economic impact on the property owner, the ultimate conclusion "necessarily requires a weighing of private and public interests" [*Agins v. City of Tiburon* (1980)]. When the government regulation prevents the owner from any economically valuable use of his property, the private interest is unquestionably substantial, but we have never before held that no public interest can outweigh it. Instead the Court's prior decisions "uniformly reject the proposition that diminution in property value standing alone, can establish a 'taking'" [*Penn Central Transportation Co. v. New York City* (1978)].

This Court repeatedly has recognized the ability of government, in certain circumstances, to regulate property without compensation, no matter how adverse the financial effect on the owner may be. More than a century ago, the Court explicitly upheld the right of States to prohibit uses of property injurious to public health, safety, or welfare without paying compensation: "A prohibition simply upon the use of property for purposes that are declared, by valid legislation, to be injurious to the health, morals, or safety of the community, cannot in any just sense, be deemed a taking or an appropriation of property" [*Mugler v. Kansas* (1887)]. . . .

The Court recognizes that "our prior opinions have suggested that "harmful or noxious uses" of property may be proscribed by government regulation without the requirement of compensation," but seeks to reconcile them with its categorical rule by claiming that the Court never has upheld a regulation when the owner alleged the loss of all economic value. Even if the Court's factual premise were correct, its understanding of the Court's cases is distorted. In none of the cases did the Court suggest that the right of a State to prohibit certain activities without paying compensation turned on the availability of some residual valuable use. Instead, the cases depended on whether the government interest was sufficient to prohibit the activity, given the significant private cost.

These cases rest on the principle that the State has full power to prohibit an owner's use of property if it is harmful to the public. [S]ince no individual has a right to use his property so as to create a nuisance or otherwise harm others, the State has not "taken" anything when it asserts its power to enjoin the nuisance-like activity." It would make no sense under this theory to suggest that an owner has a constitutionally protected right to harm others, if only he makes the proper showing of economic loss. . . .

Until today, the Court explicitly had rejected the contention that the government's power to act without paying compensation turns on whether the prohibited activity is a common law nuisance. The brewery closed in *Mugler* itself was not a common law nuisance, and the Court specifically stated that it was the role of the legislature to determine what measures would be appropriate for the protection of public health and safety.

The Court rejects the notion that the State always can prohibit uses it deems a harm to the public without granting compensation because "the distinction between 'harm-preventing' and 'benefit-conferring' regulation is often in the eye of the beholder." The Court, however, fails to explain how its proposed common-law alternative escapes the same trap.

The threshold inquiry for imposition of the Court's new rule, "deprivation of all economically valuable use," itself cannot be determined objectively. As the Court admits, whether the owner has been deprived of all economic value of his property will depend on how "property" is defined. . . .

Even more perplexing, however, is the Court's reliance on common law principles of nuisance in its quest for a value-free takings jurisprudence. In determining what is a nuisance at common law, state courts make exactly the decision that the Court finds so troubling when made by the South Carolina General Assembly today: They determine whether the use is harmful. Common law public and private nuisance law is simply a determination whether a particular use causes harm. There is nothing magical in the reasoning of judges long dead. They determined a harm in the same way as state judges and legislatures do today. If judges in the 18th and 19th centuries can distinguish a harm from a benefit, why not judges in the 20th century, and if judges can, why not legislators? There simply is no reason to believe that new interpretations of the hoary common law nuisance doctrine will be particularly "objective" or "valuefree." Once one abandons the level of generality of sic utere tuo ut alienum non laedas [you cannot use your property in a way harmful to others], one searches in vain, I think, for anything resembling a principle in the common law of nuisance.

Historically, Banning Harmful Use of Land Has Not Been Compensated

Finally, the Court justifies its new rule that the legislature may not deprive a property owner of the only economically valuable use of his land, even if the legislature finds it to be a harmful use, because such action is not part of the 'long recognized' "understandings of our citizens." These "understandings" permit such regulation only if the use is a nuisance under the common law. Any other course is "inconsistent with the historical compact recorded in the Takings Clause." It is not clear from the Court's opinion where our "historical compact" or "citizens' understanding" comes from, but it does not appear to be history.

The principle that the State should compensate individuals for property taken for public use was not widely established in America at the time of the Revolution. . . .

Even into the 19th century, state governments often felt free to take property for roads and other public projects without paying compensation to the owners. There was an obvious movement toward establishing the just compensation principle during the 19th century, but there continued to be a strong current in American legal thought that regarded compensation simply as a "bounty given . . . by the State" out of "kindness," and not out of justice. . . .

Even when courts began to consider that regulation in some situations could constitute a taking, they continued to uphold bans on particular uses without paying compensation, notwithstanding the economic impact, under the rationale that no one can obtain a vested right to injure or endanger the public. . . .

In addition, state courts historically have been less likely to find that a government action constitutes a taking when the affected land is undeveloped. According to the South Carolina court, the power of the legislature to take unimproved land without providing compensation was sanctioned by "ancient rights and principles.". . .

With similar result, the common agrarian conception of property limited owners to "natural" uses of their land prior to and during much of the 18th century. Thus, for example, the owner could build nothing on his land that would alter the natural flow of water.

Nor does history indicate any common law limit on the State's power to regulate harmful uses even to the point of destroying all economic value. Nothing in the discussions in Congress concerning the Takings Clause indicates that the Clause was limited by the common law nuisance doctrine. Common-law courts themselves rejected such an understanding. They regularly recognized that it is for the legislature to interpose, and by positive enactment to prohibit a use of property which would be injurious to the public."

In short, I find no clear and accepted "historical compact" or "understanding of our citizens" justifying the Court's new takings doctrine. Instead, the Court seems to treat history as a grab bag of principles, to be adopted where they support the

Court's theory and ignored where they do not. If the Court decided that the early common law provides the background principles for interpreting the Takings Clause, then regulation, as opposed to physical confiscation, would not be compensable. If the Court decided that the law of a later period provides the background principles, then regulation might be compensable, but the Court would have to confront the fact that legislatures regularly determined which uses were prohibited, independent of the common law, and independent of whether the uses were lawful when the owner purchased. What makes the Court's analysis unworkable is its attempt to package the law of two incompatible eras and peddle it as historical fact.

The Court makes sweeping and, in my view, misguided and unsupported changes in our takings doctrine. While it limits these changes to the most narrow subset of government regulation—those that eliminate all economic value from land—these changes go far beyond what is necessary to secure petitioner Lucas' private benefit. One hopes they do not go beyond the narrow confines the Court assigns them to today.

"If a law or regulation results in a loss of value, does the regulating agency owe you money just the same as if they physically take your land for a road?"

The Court's Ruling Brought Regulatory Takings Under the Protection of the Fifth Amendment

David Lucas

David Lucas, a real estate developer, was the plaintiff in Lucas v. South Carolina Coastal Council. *The following viewpoint is from his book about his court battles,* Lucas vs. the Green Machine. *In it he describes his reaction to the Supreme Court's decision that the state must pay him for the land on which new restrictions would not allow him to build. The state had claimed that it need not compensate Lucas because it could legally stop the use of land for a nuisance without payment, but the Court ruled that governments can prevent "nuisance" use only in situations where next-door neighbors can. There were already houses on neighboring lots, and so building new ones could not be called a nuisance, even though it could be prohibited for environmental reasons. Lucas was pleased with this ruling not only because it meant that he himself would be paid for his land, but because the Court declared that the Fifth Amendment protects all owners against total loss of their property's value through new land-use regulations.*

David Lucas, *Lucas vs. the Green Machine*. Alexander, NC: Alexander Books, 1995. pp. 230–235.

L inda [a friend] said that the decision was signed by Justice [Antonin] Scalia. I thought to myself, "That is a very good sign." Then she said three beautiful sounding words "Reversed and Remanded." Three simple words that were music to my ears. I knew enough by now about the law to understand that we had at least won something. Linda said that she would begin faxing the decision immediately.

My fax rang and the sheets began to flow down the telephone wires from Washington [D.C.] to my office in Mount Pleasant [South Carolina]. As it turned out, there were seventy two pages in Justice Scalia's majority opinion. I called Jerry [my lawyer] to tell him the news. He was just getting his copy also by facsimile, and he told me that he would call me back as soon as he understood the ruling. He did tell me that it seemed to be a six to three opinion. We had won something with one vote to spare.

Before I could finish reading my copy, the phone started to ring. It was the press. The reporters were asking for interviews and comments. I told them that I would have to call them back after I had read the opinion. I was almost too excited to focus my eyes on the pages. Justice Scalia had prevailed. He and the majority of the Justices had ruled that the State of South Carolina had no more power to stop me from building on my land than my next door neighbor did. My neighbor had the right to stop me from doing anything on my property that was considered a common law nuisance, and the state had the same right as my neighbor. However, it did not have more of a right than my neighbor, even though the South Carolina legislature had tried to give itself more power through the 1988 Beach Front Management Act. The Supreme Court ruled that the state could not avoid compensating me by simply passing a new law and declaring a previously lawful act a nuisance.

The State Must Pay

The majority had ruled that the state had to prove that my building a house on the beach was a nuisance under the existing nuisance laws of the state to avoid paying compensation. If they could not prove that the building of a house was a common law nuisance, then the state would owe me just compensation. This was exactly what the Fifth Amendment said. In the court's opinion, the state would have a difficult time proving that building a house on my lots was a nuisance, since there were houses all around my lots and the state did not consider them a nuisance. I felt elated and vindicated.

This was the heart of the ruling. It disagreed with the police power's argument that the state had made. The state had argued that any legitimate use of the state police powers exempted them from having to compensate the owner. The United States Supreme Court said, No. Only if the police power was stopping a common law nuisance already in common acceptance, would it exempt the state from payment.

As to valuation, (how much money the state owed me) the court also ruled that when a regulation takes all economic value, that constitutes a unique category of taking, and requires compensation from the regulating body without meeting any other tests. This was good for me, but this language was to be used by property rights opponents to cloud the ruling for others. They soon began to interpret this part of the ruling as requiring a one hundred percent devaluation before compensation is required. Justice Scalia tried to warn government regulators to beware of thinking that all economic value must be gone before the court would consider that reduction in value as a taking. In footnote number eight he said:

> "Justice [John Paul] Stevens criticizes the 'deprivation of all economically beneficial use' rule as 'wholly arbitrary,' in that '[the] landowner whose property is diminished in value 95 percent recovers nothing,' while the landowner who suffers a complete elimination of value 'recovers the land's full value.'

This analysis errs in its assumption that the landowner whose deprivation is one step short of complete is not entitled to compensation. Such an owner might not be able to claim the benefit of our categorical formulation, but, as we have acknowledged time and again, '[t]he economic impact of the regulation on the claimant and . . . the extent to which the regulation has interfered with distinct investment-backed expectations' are keenly relevant to takings analysis generally [*Penn Central Transportation Co. v. New York City* (1978)]. It is true that, in at least some cases, the landowner with 95 percent loss will get nothing, while the landowner with total loss will recover in full; but that occasional result is no more strange than the gross disparity between the landowner, whose premises are taken for a highway (who recovers in full), and the landowner whose property is reduced to 5 percent of its former value by the highway (who recovers nothing). Takings law is full of these 'all-or-nothing' situations."

This was good news. I was happy with the opinion. We had been hoping for a plain reinstatement of the lower court ruling, money damages and all. That would have ended the matter and made the law and the Constitution very clear. But that was not the way it was going to be. There were definitely going to be more courts, and more lawyers, and more legal fees involved, in this most interesting time in my life (there is an old Arabian curse that says, "May your life be long *and* interesting"). Still, a victory is sweet and this was a victory on all the legal and constitutional points we had argued.

The Dissenting Opinion Was Disappointing

My enthusiasm was tempered somewhat when I got around to reading the dissenting opinion of Justice [Harry] Blackmun. His opening sentence was, "Today the court has launched a missile to kill a mouse." Well, maybe from his point of view, but this mouse was bringing in the modern version of the economic bubonic plague and deserved to be destroyed by any means possible.

As it has turned out, this mouse refuses to admit that it is dead. After reading Justice Blackmun's writing, I could only shake my head and wonder at what lengths some people go to, to twist and torture simple reason. Instead of getting angry, I felt sorry for this man. How could someone, so dedicated to other civil rights, not recognize that the Fifth Amendment allows people to acquire property, and therefore, also acquire relative independence from economic coercion, and that this is the underpinning for all other civil rights. Of course, if I had lost the case, I would have certainly had different emotions and pity would not have been one of them.

There was much more in those seventy-two pages than I have room to give you here. . . . In my view, the court had done an excellent job in settling the question, "Can a regulation result in a compensable taking?" Or, in layman's terms, if a law or regulation results in a loss of value, does the regulating agency owe you money just the same as if they physically take your land for a road? The court had answered; yes. This was the heart of the ruling in my case. Regulatory takings had now been brought firmly under the umbrella protection of the Fifth Amendment of the United States Constitution.

"The tragedy of Lucas *is that the Court has told governments, in effect, 'you can take and you won't have to pay as long as you don't take it all.'"*

The Court's Ruling on Compensation for Land-Use Regulations May Not Help Property Owners

Henry N. Butler

Henry N. Butler is the executive director of the Searle Center at Northwestern University School of Law. In the following viewpoint, he explains that although the Supreme Court ruled in favor of David Lucas in Lucas v. South Carolina Coastal Council, *the decision may not be of much help to other property owners because it was specifically limited to situations in which government action has ruled a piece of property valueless. The Court held that the takings clause of the Fifth Amendment does not apply when a taking is only partial. In most cases, Butler points out, government land-use restrictions do not take away all of a property's value; landowners can still put it to some kind of use. So in effect, what the decision did was to tell governments how to write regulations in such a way as to not have to reimburse the property owner.*

The Fifth Amendment to the United States Constitution concludes with the Takings Clause—"nor shall private property be taken for public use without just compensation."

Henry N. Butler, "Regulatory Takings After *Lucas*," *Regulation: The Cato Review of Business & Government*, Fall 1993. www.cato.org. Copyright © 1993 Cato Institute. All rights reserved. Reproduced by permission.

There are several common-sense reasons why this clause was included in the Bill of Rights. First, protection of property rights (through the public use and compensation requirements) encourages private investment and promotes economic prosperity. Second, compensation is equitable in the sense that no one individual or group is forced to bear a disproportionately large share of the costs of a government program. Third, the public use requirement could limit the scope of government activities to those that involve primarily public, rather than private (special interest), benefits. Fourth, the compensation requirement serves as an important restraint by requiring the government to pay for all the resources that it commands. Although this list of rationales is not necessarily exhaustive, it does suggest that a consideration of these rationales could provide some guidance to the application and interpretation of the Takings Clause. Unfortunately, judicial interpretation of constitutional provisions is never so straightforward.

Like many areas of constitutional jurisprudence, judicial interpretation of the Takings Clause has created a confused and baffling body of law. For example, the Supreme Court has emasculated the "public use" requirement to the point that "public use" means whatever the taking government says is a public use. Nevertheless, when government physically invades private property, it is clear that a taking has occurred and that compensation is owed to the property holder.

What is not clear is the extent to which the Takings Clause offers property owners protection against reductions in property value caused by government regulations—so-called regulatory takings. In many instances, especially land-use regulations, the effect of regulations is to impose substantial costs on some property owners in the name of achieving what the government has determined to be a public benefit. Thus, many regulatory-induced reductions in property value are potentially characterized as takings subject to the just compensation provisions of the Takings Clause. Indeed, compensation for a typical regulatory taking would seem to fit within the primary justifications for the Takings Clause—encouraging investment, preventing inequitable treatment, and restraining government.

Nevertheless, this approach to property rights and regulatory takings offers too much—almost every government action impacts property values, and it would be totally unworkable to require compensation every time a government action causes a diminution in value. But that does not mean that there should be no protection against regulatory takings. Proponents of greater property rights protection have long recognized the need for a principled approach to regulatory takings that is consistent with the overall purposes of the Takings Clause.

Property Rights in the Reagan-Bush Supreme Court

Prospects for greater protection for private property owners looked bright as the Reagan-Bush appointees took control of the Supreme Court. However, property rights proponents' expectations have been treated to a roller coaster ride by recent Supreme Court decisions. Beginning with three cases in 1987, the Court seemed to signal the start of a new era in which greater protection from regulatory takings would guarantee property owners compensation in the event that government actions reduced the value of their property. In fact, the 1987 decisions prompted President Reagan to issue an Executive Order calling for a "regulatory takings review" of all new federal regulations.

The prospect of greater protection of property rights appeared even brighter when the Supreme Court agreed to review the South Carolina case of *Lucas v. South Carolina Coastal Council*. Anticipation of an important decision affording greater protection against government action was reflected in numerous law review articles and the popular press. But even before *Lucas* was announced in 1992, the Court lowered expectations with its decision in *Yee v. City of Escondido*, which rejected a property owner's efforts to expand the Court's takings test to encompass regulation of mobile home parks. The Court refused to consider the petitioner's argument that although no actual physical invasion occurred, the county ordinance amounted to a regulatory taking because it deprived mobile home park owners of the economic use of their property. The Court described the regulatory takings analysis in terms of an ad hoc balancing test that "necessarily entails complex factual assessments of the purposes and economic effects of government actions." That is not the type of language that promotes and protects private property, but things got worse in *Lucas*.

The facts in *Lucas* are straightforward. David Lucas, a real estate developer, bought two beachfront lots on a South Carolina barrier island in anticipation of building vacation homes as was then permitted by all relevant regulatory bodies. The South Carolina Legislature then enacted the South Carolina Beachfront Management Act, which prevented Lucas from building on his property. A state trial court found that the state's action was a taking because it rendered the property "valueless" and ordered compensation. The South Carolina Supreme Court reversed the decision on the ground that no compensation is owed under the Takings Clause regardless of the regulation's effect on the property's value when a regulation is designed to prevent "harmful or noxious uses" of property. The notion that building a home at the beach is a "harmful or noxious" use of property would strike most people as strange or even bizarre, but the South Carolina Supreme Court accepted the legislature's determination that building additional homes would threaten existing homes and the delicate environmental system of the barrier islands. Had the South Carolina decision been upheld, Mr. Lucas would have been faced with the loss of over $1 million.

The U.S. Supreme Court's decision to grant *certiorari* [review] in *Lucas* created a great deal of excitement among property rights proponents as well as a great deal of concern among environmentalists. For property rights proponents, *Lucas* was a good case in the sense that the South Carolina Supreme Court's decision seemed so inequitable that the U.S. Supreme Court was bound to offer some relief. *Lucas* also presented an opportunity to develop a coherent theory of regulatory takings that would act as a real constraint on regulatory activity. On the other hand, environmentalists were concerned that the Court, in granting relief to Lucas, would rein in the regulatory demands of the environmental lobby. As it turned out, all the glee and hand wringing were for naught.

The Distinction Between Total and Partial Takings

The Supreme Court's decision in *Lucas* was a major disappointment because the opinion unnecessarily limited its impact to unusual situations where the regulatory taking renders the property "valueless." Justice Antonin Scalia, writing for a majority of six, delineated a boundary between compensable and non-compensable land-use regulations based on the distinction between total and partial regulatory takings. Justice Scalia held that the Takings Clause reached only those land-use restrictions that deprived the owner of "all economically beneficial uses" of property. That statement was sufficient to overturn the South Carolina Supreme Court, but it failed to offer any improvement to the law of regulatory takings because most regulatory takings do not render the affected property "valueless." Thus, land-use regulations ostensibly adopted to promote some articulated state interest will not require compensation to injured landowners so long as there is not a total taking or a physical invasion of the property.

The distinction between total and partial regulatory takings is the most troublesome aspect of Justice Scalia's opinion.

The distinction is arbitrary and inconsistent with the purposes of the Takings Clause. For the typical landowner, the distinction between total and partial takings represents a difference in relative magnitude of loss for any given piece of property, but makes little sense in terms of a landowner bearing a disproportionately large share of the burden of creating some public benefit. Under the *Lucas* Court's total/partial distinction, one landowner's non-compensable partial taking may be a much larger dollar loss than another landowner's compensable total taking. In this regard, the total/partial distinction seems arbitrary and unsound.

Moreover, the total/partial distinction for regulatory takings was not necessary in light of earlier Supreme Court decisions involving partial physical takings. For example, in the 1933 case of *Jacobs v. United States*, farmers sued the federal government to recover compensation for the occasional flooding of their property that was caused by the construction of a dam by the federal government. The Supreme Court ruled that there had been a partial taking of the lands in question, for which the government was required to make compensation under the Fifth Amendment. Many years later, in *Griggs v. Allegheney County* (1962), the Court addressed the partial physical taking of air space over land. In that case, the county established an airport next to residential property, making it unsuitable for residential use. The Court required payment of compensation even though the property could be used for non-residential or commercial purposes—that is, even though the property was not made valueless. Thus, it is clear from an analogous area of Takings jurisprudence that Supreme Court precedent did not prohibit Justice Scalia from requiring compensation for partial regulatory takings.

The most plausible explanation for why Justice Scalia adopted the total/partial distinction is that requiring compensation for partial takings would have laid the foundation for an all-out assault on other partial regulatory takings, such as zoning restrictions and rent control. *Lucas* offered a potential vehicle for such a dramatic change in property rights protection because most of the Justices did not really believe that Lucas had lost all economically beneficial use of his property. That is, *Lucas* really involved a partial taking, but Justice Scalia chose to adopt the South Carolina trial court's characterization of it as a total taking and use the total/partial distinction to limit the scope of the decision. Unfortunately, the *Lucas* opinion gives legislators and lower courts plenty of guidance about how to avoid finding a regulatory taking.

As disappointing as the *Lucas* holding might be to proponents of property rights, it is useful to keep some perspective on the decision by considering Justice [Harry] Blackmun's view of Mr. Lucas's unfortunate treatment at the hands of the South Carolina Legislature. In a strong dissent to Justice Scalia's majority opinion, Justice Blackmun concluded that "even assuming that petitioner's property was rendered valueless, the risk inherent in investments of the sort made by petitioner, the generality of the Act, and the compelling purpose motivating the South Carolina Legislature persuade me that the Act did not effect a taking of petitioner's property." Real estate developers, like Mr. Lucas, are accustomed to the financial risk involved in their business. Owners of beachfront homes, like Mr. Lucas hoped to become, are well aware of the risks of storms and hurricanes. However, just because people are willing to incur those types of risks, it does not follow that they willingly accept the risk that the legislature can take their property with no prospect of compensation. Under Blackmun's view, the biggest risk—apparently an "inherent" risk—of owning property is that the legislature will destroy its value free of any obligation to compensate the victim. This brings real meaning to the saying "When the legislature is in session, there is no such thing as an insurable interest."

Lucas not only failed to meet its potential to provide more protection for property owners, it also instructed governments how to avoid paying the full costs of regulatory takings. The tragedy of *Lucas* is that the Court has told governments, in effect, "you can take and you won't have to pay as long as you don't take it all."

Casual observation of politics at any level of government teaches us that we should never underestimate the ability of politicians and interest groups to take advantage of every opportunity to use political force to transfer wealth. But Supreme Court opinions continue to reflect a naive view of politics and the American democratic process. Nowhere is that naivete more evident than in *Lucas*. The *Lucas* decision creates a clear road map for how legislators should write legislation to avoid regulatory takings claims. As a result, we may have seen the last regulatory taking—at least according to Justice Scalia's definition—but we can expect to see even more legislative intrusions on property rights. . . .

Postscript

On remand, the South Carolina Supreme Court ordered the state of South Carolina to purchase the Lucas property. As the new owner of a previously "worthless" piece of property, the state has decided to enter the real estate development business and has offered the property for sale as residential sites. Presumably, the state has changed its land-use restrictions to allow the development. This role reversal demonstrates that actions that may appear to be in the public interest when they are "free"—that is, when the political decision makers don't bear the costs—are not necessarily attractive government programs once the political decision makers must bear the budgetary costs of their actions. It is difficult to find a better example of how protection for owners of private property serves to restrain the growth of government.

"The potential impact of such a ruling on environmental and other regulation that limits the ways in which owners can use their land is enormous."

The Court's Ruling May Open the Way to Future Decisions That Restrict Environmental Legislation

Louise A. Halper

Louise A. Halper is a professor of law at the Washington and Lee University School of Law in Lexington, Virginia, and a former environmental litigator for the state of New York. In the following viewpoint, she explains the Supreme Court's ruling in Lucas v. South Carolina Coastal Council, *which held that the government has no more power to stop specific land uses without compensating the owners than neighboring property owners do. If owners use their land in a way harmful to neighbors, they do not receive any money for stopping, but if the government restricts its use for some other reason and it becomes worthless, the owners must be paid for their loss. Although this ruling applies only if the loss it total, Halper suggests that a future Court might make it applicable to partial losses, which would have a major impact on the enactment of land use and environmental regulations.*

In 1992, the Supreme Court of the United States decided *Lucas v. South Carolina Coastal Council*, an eagerly awaited test case of environmental and land-use regulation. The court ruled, for the first time in almost 75 years, that a state law was unconstitutional because, although it did not physically take property, it reduced the land's value and provided no compensation to the owner. The potential impact of such a ruling on environmental and other regulation that limits the ways in which owners can use their land is enormous.

The Fifth Amendment of the U.S. Constitution bars the government from confiscating private property. That is not to say owners cannot be forced to give up their property, but they must be fairly compensated. In essence, the U.S. government has the power, known as eminent domain, to force a citizen to sell. If your land is needed for a road, for example, you cannot, by refusing to sell, require the road to be built elsewhere. But when your land is taken, you must receive its fair market value in exchange for your loss of its use.

But what if the event that causes the loss is not a physical intrusion but a law or regulation that reduces the value of your property? Are you entitled to compensation on the grounds that the regulation amounts to confiscation—or what lawyers call a taking—because of the loss of your property's value? For many years, the Supreme Court did not recognize the concept of a "regulatory taking," or a law that so diminished the value of property as to constitute the equivalent of a physical taking. If there were no transfer of title or physical invasion, there was no taking. Because relatively little regulation was enacted in the 19th century, the court's refusal to compensate for a regulation's effect on property was not pressing. But with the birth of the regulatory state and particularly with the bureaucratization of land use and land-use planning after World War I, the question of whether loss of value could be a taking emerged. . . .

The question of how to make the difficult distinction between a regulatory taking and a regulation that coincidentally lowers the value of property has simmered for the [past] 70 years. . . . During that period, zoning ordinances, historic landmark designations, and environmental legislation—all of them regulations that affect the value of real property—have been passed by legislatures and withstood legal challenge. Indeed, up until the decision in *Lucas* a land-use regulation had never been ruled a taking.

That is really the nub of the *Lucas* case. For many conservatives the entire vast suite of regulations limiting, restricting, and molding the ways in which property can be used is a source of irritation and anger. In the prelude to what was called the Reagan Revolution, sentiment built among conservatives to halt and perhaps reverse the post-New Deal regulatory regime that so affected property values. Many believed that the time was ripe for a re-evaluation of the overregulation of property. With a newly conservative Supreme Court, it appeared that a reversal of the regulatory state might be in the offing; the court, led in this effort by Justice Antonin Scalia, seemed poised to reconsider past precedents. Property rights advocates worked to find cases in which the court could announce, on the basis of clear and easily understood facts, new principles restricting the power of government to reduce property value without compensation.

Lucas's Property Became Worthless

Lucas, seemed to be that clear case. Before South Carolina's passage of a new law, David Lucas's property was worth $1 million; afterwards, zero. In 1986, Lucas, a real estate developer, had paid almost a million dollars for two oceanfront lots on the Isle of Palms in South Carolina. When he bought them, both lots were zoned for single-family residential construction. Two years later, before Lucas took any significant steps toward construction, the South Carolina legislature changed the rules regulating coastal construction. The construction line was moved inland; Lucas's lots, on each of which he had planned to build a house, were seaward of that line.

Lucas sued, alleging that the Beachfront Management Act of 1988 (BMA) constituted a permanent and total taking of the value of his property without just compensation. The trial court found that Lucas had suffered a total diminution of the value of his property and concluded that a regulatory taking had occurred. When the Coastal Council appealed, the Supreme Court of South Carolina reversed the lower court's ruling. BMA, the court said, was passed to prevent serious public harm; its limitations constituted a permissible restriction of Lucas's use of the property. Lucas subsequently appealed to the Supreme Court of the United States.

To the Supreme Court, Lucas made the argument that any regulation that works a total diminution of value is a taking. Although Scalia, who wrote the opinion for the majority, was sympathetic, Lucas's simple and appealing argument had a serious flaw. If the entire value of Lucas's property were in its use for a purpose that was decidedly dangerous or unhealthy, would the state still have to compensate Lucas if it passed a law that barred such a use? If, for example, Lucas had used his land as a toxic waste dump and now could make no other use of it, would the state have to compensate Lucas if it banned toxic waste dumps on the shore? Lucas's argument was precisely that.

A Property Owner Cannot Maintain a Nuisance

There is a very long common-law tradition, however, that the state has a responsibility to safeguard its citizens' health and welfare and that it may, on that basis, limit the uses of private property. If the state decided to ban toxic waste dumps as a threat to public health, Lucas would not be entitled to compensation even if he had no alternative use for his land and the value of the land was reduced to zero. Neither Lucas nor any other property owner can maintain a nuisance, a use that threatens public health and safety. This reasoning is known as the "nuisance exception" to the takings doctrine. The South Carolina Coastal Council argued that BMA was sustainable under that exception because it was designed to protect the public by avoiding harm to the shoreline. Because BMA was passed pursuant to the state's police power to prevent harm to the public, Lucas need not be compensated for the loss of value caused by the new construction line, even if that loss were total.

Scalia rejected South Carolina's argument. He said that, although the nuisance exception had been recognized for many years, it was too problematic to apply to a total loss of value. How can one tell if the state, in barring certain uses of property as a nuisance, is really acting to safeguard the health and welfare of its citizens? Perhaps the legislature is simply using health and safety as the politically popular substitute for making the public pay for a benefit and forcing an individual landowner to bear alone a burden that should be divided among all taxpayers. In *Lucas*, for example, there was some evidence that the legislature's aim in passing the Beachfront Management Act was not to safeguard the public but to promote tourism. Promoting tourism, like building a road, may be a legitimate public purpose, but it provides the public with a benefit, rather than preventing a harm. Thus, if undertaken, promoting tourism must be paid for. Should citizens take the legislature's word that a regulation constitutes an attempt to eliminate a public burden, or should the courts be asked to determine whether the "real" purpose of the law is to provide a low-cost public benefit?

The latter course is fraught with the danger of confrontation between legislature and judiciary. It has not been thought wise, at least since the New Deal era, to allow courts to second-guess legislatures with respect to the substance of regulation.

Were the courts allowed to do so now, years of land-use planning, environmental regulation, and zoning might be challenged and fall. And yet, said Scalia, if "the uses of private property [are] subject to unbridled, uncompensated qualification under the police power," private property will eventually disappear. Thus, the problem posed by Lucas, from the point of view of a majority sympathetic to his loss of property value, was to fashion an opinion that allowed the court to find a regulatory taking—in the face of the state legislature's argument that its statute was a legitimate exercise of its police power—without at the same time giving courts the power to sit as super-legislatures, overseeing every piece of land-use regulation.

Scalia's escape from the dilemma began with his denial of its existence. The difference between eliminating a danger to the public and conferring an uncompensated benefit upon the public is "in the eye of the beholder," he wrote. What looks to a member of the public like the prevention of harm may look to the affected landowner like the securing of a public benefit. The declaration that the burden/benefit distinction is indeterminate is a dramatic change in legal doctrine. It had been understood for at least a century that there was a difference—perhaps not a bright line, but nonetheless a discernible one—between the state's exercise of eminent domain—that is, the compensable taking of property for a desirable public use—and its uncompensable exercise of its police power to prevent harm. Nonetheless, said Scalia, it is impossible to come up with a coherent or principled distinction between the two.

A Property Owner Cannot Interfere with a Neighbor's Rights

Instead of engaging in the doomed effort of distinguishing burden from benefit to answer the question of whether a particular regulation "goes too far," Scalia turned to the law governing the relationships of private landowners. An ancient principle of the common law is that the right to use one's property is limited by the equal right of one's neighbor to an equivalent freedom of use. For example, if your neighbor attempts to use her property for a toxic waste dump that threatens to poison your property, you may ask a court to bar that use, and you will probably succeed. Thus, said Scalia, the legislature too may bar such a use. A use that illegitimately interferes with a neighbor is not a right that a landowner holds by virtue of her ownership. On the other hand, another neighbor may have peculiar taste, but unless you can buy him out, you cannot keep him from painting his house in purple and yellow stripes because his choice of colors does not affect any right you have to use your own property.

According to the *Lucas* holding, then, the inquiry to be made about any legislation that causes a total diminution in the value of someone's land is whether the use lost is one that the landowner would be entitled to maintain if a neighbor tried to stop him. "Where the State seeks to sustain regulation that deprives land of all economically beneficial use, we think it may resist compensation only if the logically antecedent inquiry into the nature of the owner's estate shows that the proscribed use interests were not part of his title to begin with. If Ann, a landowner, could go to court and, under the common law of nuisance, stop Bill, her neighbor, from what he was doing, then the state too could halt Bill's use. If Ann could not win a court order to stop Bill but could only stop him by purchasing his use, then the state too must pay to buy out Bill. The state has no power to bar any use of Bill's property that the common law would not allow Ann to halt.

Lucas, holds that the extent of the state's exercise of the police power—its power to protect public health and safety—and the individual landowner's power to contain or halt a use harmful to her are identical. There can be no regulation on behalf of public interests any broader than the interests of abutters. Where private parties can restrain each other's uses, the state may do so; where private parties can extinguish each other's uses only by purchase, the state too must expend funds. In short, the police power is the public equivalent of the common law of private nuisance. . . .

Scalia, challenged by Justice John Paul Stevens to explain why a 100-percent loss would be compensated but a 95-percent loss would not, could give no principled reason for restricting the scope of the opinion. His silence suggests that the way might be open for an even more conservative court to restrict further the power of legislatures to enact land-use and environmental regulations.

CHAPTER 2

The Government Need Not Pay for Land if Its Use Is Temporarily Restricted

Case Overview

Tahoe-Sierra Preservation Council v. Tahoe Regional Planning Agency (2002)

Lake Tahoe, located on the border between California and Nevada, is noted as one of the most beautiful lakes in the world. It is a large, deep blue lake surrounded by pine-clad mountains, and is especially renowned for the clarity of its water, which nineteenth-century author Mark Twain described as "not merely transparent, but dazzlingly, brilliantly so." In 1872 he wrote, "The bottom was so perfectly distinct that the boat seemed floating in the air! Yes, where it was even eighty feet deep. Every little pebble was distinct, every speckled trout, every hand's-breadth of sand."

A hundred years later, in 1972, Lake Tahoe's water was still clear—but not, people feared, for much longer. The area had become a more and more popular place not only for short summer vacations, but for skiing in the winter and for year-round retirement living. Resorts and homes had multiplied; on the Nevada side, there was even a high-rise gambling casino. Experts predicted that so much development, especially the impact of buildings and paved parking areas, would lead to the growth of algae in the lake, causing it to lose its clarity and become not blue, but green. Therefore, the Tahoe Regional Planning Agency (TRPA) adopted a land-use ordinance designed to limit the amount of land that could be covered by impervious surfaces. This proved to have little effect on the number of new homes built, and so TRPA began developing a plan for more comprehensive environmental restrictions. In 1981 it imposed a moratorium on construction of new residences, which was originally intended to be brief but which was stretched through successive ordinances to last for six years.

Owners of empty lots in the area had bought the land with the understanding that they could build retirement or vacation homes. Some had put all their savings into it. They banded together and sued, saying that because this moratorium deprived them of use of their property, it was a taking under the takings clause of the Fifth Amendment to the Constitution, and they should therefore be compensated. But is restriction of land use a taking if it is merely temporary? This question, complicated by the fact that successive relatively short moratoria were involved, was considered several times in various forms by the District Court and by the Court of Appeals. Ultimately the Court of Appeals ruled that a temporary restriction is not a taking, but a number of the judges dissented; they maintained that this decision was not consistent with the 1992 precedent set by *Lucas v. South Carolina Coastal Council.* The U.S. Supreme Court then agreed to review the case.

The attorney that represented the TRPA before the Supreme Court was John Roberts, who several years later was appointed to be its Chief Justice. "A temporary ban on development doesn't render property valueless," he pointed out during the oral arguments. "If you have two parcels of property, one subject to a permanent ban on use, and the other subject to a temporary ban, it is true . . . the permanent ban could be made temporary and the temporary ban could be made permanent, but you're not going to pay the same price for both of those parcels of property. The one that's subject to the temporary ban is going to have a higher market value, reflecting the fact that future uses are available, or will be available or not, depending on the plan that's ultimately adopted."

Largely for that reason, the Court ruled that the *Lucas* precedent was not applicable in this case. Furthermore, the majority felt that to require planners to pay for temporary moratoria would lead them to make hurried, unwise decisions about land use. There should not be a categorical rule about temporary takings, it declared; the circumstances of each case should be considered. But the dissenters pointed out that if temporary bans on building were not considered takings, then all a government would have to do to avoid paying would be to label every ban "temporary" and then keep extending its termination date.

Everyone agreed that it was important to preserve Lake Tahoe. That was in the best interests of the landowners as well as the public since their land would certainly lose value if the lake's beauty were destroyed. However, the dissenting justices declared that the cost of preservation should be borne by everyone—that is, by the taxpayers—rather than only by the people who were forbidden to build on property they had bought with the expectation of living there.

"A rule that required compensation for every delay in the use of property would render routine government processes prohibitively expensive or encourage hasty decision-making."

The Court's Decision: A Moratorium on Land Development Is Not the Same as Permanent Loss of Property Value

John Paul Stevens

John Paul Stevens is, as of 2008, the oldest and longest-serving member of the Supreme Court, and is generally considered to be the leader of its liberal faction. The following is his majority opinion in Tahoe-Sierra Preservation Council v. Tahoe Regional Planning Agency, *a case in which landowners who had been denied the use of their property near Lake Tahoe by environmental regulations claimed compensation under the takings clause of the Fifth Amendment. Justice Stevens explains the Court's reasoning in ruling that the temporary ban on use of their land was not a taking, and that therefore, the government did not have to pay any compensation. The precedent of* Lucas v. South Carolina Coastal Council *in 1992 was not applicable, he says, because they did not lose all economically beneficial uses of the land. Furthermore, the Court decided that in the case of temporary restrictions, there should not be any categorical rule as to whether there are takings; the circumstances of each case*

John Paul Stevens, majority opinion, *Tahoe-Sierra Preservation Council v. Tahoe Regional Planning Agency*, U.S. Supreme Court, April 23, 2002.

should be considered. And it is important, Justice Stevens points out, to protect the ability of land-use planners to make well-reasoned decisions without being rushed by the prospect of having to pay property owners for the delay.

When the government physically takes possession of an interest in property for some public purpose, it has a categorical duty to compensate the former owner, regardless of whether the interest that is taken constitutes an entire parcel or merely a part thereof. Thus, compensation is mandated when a leasehold is taken and the government occupies the property for its own purposes, even though that use is temporary. Similarly, when the government appropriates part of a rooftop in order to provide cable TV access for apartment tenants, or when its planes use private airspace to approach a government airport, it is required to pay for that share no matter how small. But a government regulation that merely prohibits landlords from evicting tenants unwilling to pay a higher rent, that bans certain private uses of a portion of an owner's property, or that forbids the private use of certain airspace, does not constitute a categorical taking. "The first category of cases requires courts to apply a clear rule; the second necessarily entails complex factual assessments of the purposes and economic effects of government actions" [*Yee v. Escondido* (1992)].

This longstanding distinction between acquisitions of property for public use, on the one hand, and regulations prohibiting private uses, on the other, makes it inappropriate to treat cases involving physical takings as controlling precedents for the evaluation of a claim that there has been a "regulatory taking," and vice versa. For the same reason that we do not ask whether a physical appropriation advances a substantial government interest or whether it deprives the owner of all economically valuable use, we do not apply our precedent from the physical takings context to regulatory takings claims. Land-use regulations are ubiquitous and most of them impact property values in some tangential way—often in completely unanticipated ways. Treating them all as *per se* takings would transform government regulation into a luxury few governments could afford. By contrast, physical appropriations are relatively rare, easily identified, and usually represent a greater affront to individual property rights. . . .

Perhaps recognizing this fundamental distinction, petitioners wisely do not place all their emphasis on analogies to physical takings cases. Instead, they rely principally on our decision in *Lucas v. South Carolina Coastal Council* (1992)—a regulatory takings case that, nevertheless, applied a categorical rule—to argue that the *Penn Central* [*Transportation Co. v. New York City* (1978)] framework is inapplicable here. A brief review of some of the cases that led to our decision in *Lucas*, however, will help to explain why the holding in that case does not answer the question presented here.

As we noted in *Lucas*, it was Justice Holmes' opinion in *Pennsylvania Coal Co. v. Mahon* [herein referred to as *Mahon* (1992) that gave birth to our regulatory takings jurisprudence. In subsequent opinions, we have repeated and consistently endorsed Holmes' observation that "if regulation goes too far it will be recognized as a taking." Justice Holmes did not provide a standard for determining when a regulation goes "too far," but he did reject the view expressed in Justice Brandeis' dissent that there could not be a taking because the property remained in the possession of the owner and had not been appropriated or used by the public. After *Mahon*, neither a physical appropriation nor a public use has ever been a necessary component of a "regulatory taking."

In the decades following that decision, we have "generally eschewed" any set formula for determining how far is too far, choosing instead to engage in "'essentially ad hoc, factual inquiries.'" Indeed, we still resist the temptation to adopt *per se* rules in our cases involving partial regulatory takings preferring to examine "a number of factors" rather than a simple "mathematically precise" formula. . . .

Since "Lucas had no reason to proceed on a 'temporary taking' theory at trial," we decided the case on the permanent taking theory that both the trial court and the State Supreme Court had addressed.

The *Lucas* Holding Does Not Apply to This Case

The categorical rule that we applied in *Lucas* states that compensation is required when a regulation deprives an owner of "*all* economically beneficial uses" of his land. Under that rule, a statute that "wholly eliminated the value" of Lucas' fee simple title clearly qualified as a taking. But our holding was limited to "the extraordinary circumstance when *no* productive or economically beneficial use of land is permitted." The emphasis on the word "no" in the text of the opinion was, in effect, reiterated in a footnote explaining that the categorical rule would not apply if the diminution in value were 95 percent instead of 100 percent. Anything less than a "complete elimination of value," or a "total loss," the Court acknowledged, would require the kind of analysis applied in *Penn Central*. . . .

Petitioners seek to bring this case under the rule announced in *Lucas* by arguing that we can effectively sever a 32-month segment from the remainder of each landowner's fee simple estate, and then ask whether that segment has been taken in its entirety by the moratoria. Of course, defining the property interest taken in terms of the very regulation being challenged is circular. With property so divided, every delay would become a total ban; the moratorium and the normal permit process alike would constitute categorical takings. Petitioners' "conceptual severance" argument is unavailing because it ignores *Penn Central*'s admonition that in regulatory takings cases we must focus on "the parcel as a whole." . . . Thus, the District Court erred when it disaggregated petitioners' property into temporal segments corresponding to the regulations at issue and then analyzed whether petitioners were deprived of all economically viable use during each period. The starting point for the court's analysis should have been to ask whether there was a total taking of the entire parcel; if not, then *Penn Central* was the proper framework.

An interest in real property is defined by the metes and bounds that describe its geographic dimensions and the term of years that describes the temporal aspect of the owner's interest. Both dimensions must be considered if the interest is to be viewed in its entirety. Hence, a permanent deprivation of the owner's use of the entire area is a taking of "the parcel as a whole," whereas a temporary restriction that merely causes a diminution in value is not. Logically, a fee simple estate cannot be rendered valueless by a temporary prohibition on economic use, because the property will recover value as soon as the prohibition is lifted. . . .

Neither *Lucas*, nor *First English* [*Evangelical Lutheran Church of Glendale v. County of Los Angeles* (1987)] nor any of our other regulatory takings cases compels us to accept petitioners' categorical submission. In fact, these cases make clear that the categorical rule in *Lucas* was carved out for the "extraordinary case" in which a regulation permanently deprives property of all value; the default rule remains that, in the regulatory taking context, we require a more fact specific inquiry. . . .

The Circumstances of Each Case Must Be Considered

The ultimate constitutional question is whether the concepts of "fairness and justice" that underlie the Takings Clause will be better served by . . . categorical rules or by a *Penn Central* inquiry into all of the relevant circumstances in particular cases. From that perspective, the extreme categorical rule that any deprivation of all economic use, no matter how brief, constitutes a compensable taking surely cannot be sustained. Petitioners' broad submission would apply to numerous "normal delays in obtaining building permits, changes in zoning ordinances, variances, and the like," as well as to orders temporarily prohibiting access to crime scenes, businesses that violate health codes, fire-damaged buildings, or other areas that we cannot now foresee. Such a rule would undoubtedly require changes in numerous practices that have long been considered permissible exercises of the police power. As Justice Holmes warned in *Mahon*, "[g]overnment hardly could go on if to some extent values incident to property could not be diminished without paying for every such change in the general law." A rule that required compensation for every delay in the use of property would render routine government processes prohibitively expensive or encourage hasty decision-making. Such an important change in the law should be the product of legislative rulemaking rather than adjudication.

More importantly, for reasons set out at some length by Justice [Sandra Day] O'Connor in her concurring opinion in *Palazzolo v. Rhode Island* [(2001)], we are persuaded that the better approach to claims that a regulation has effected a temporary taking "requires careful examination and weighing of all the relevant circumstance." . . .

In rejecting petitioners' *per se* rule, we do not hold that the temporary nature of a land-use restriction precludes finding that it effects a taking; we simply recognize that it should not be given exclusive significance one way or the other.

A narrower rule that excluded the normal delays associated with processing permits, or that covered only delays of more than a year, would certainly have a less severe impact on prevailing practices, but it would still impose serious financial constraints on the planning process. Unlike the "extraordinary circumstance" in which the government deprives a property owner of all economic use, moratoria like Ordinance 81-5 and Resolution 83-21 are used widely among land-use planners to preserve the status quo while formulating a more permanent development strategy. In fact, the consensus in the planning community appears to be that moratoria, or "interim development controls" as they are often called, are an essential tool of successful development. Yet even the weak version of petitioners' categorical rule would treat these interim measures as takings regardless of the good faith of the planners, the reasonable expectations of the landowners, or the actual impact of the moratorium on property values.

The interest in facilitating informed decision-making by regulatory agencies counsels against adopting a *per se* rule that would impose such severe costs on their deliberations. Otherwise, the financial constraints of compensating property owners during a moratorium may force officials to rush through the planning process or to abandon the practice altogether. To the extent that communities are forced to abandon using moratoria, landowners will have incentives to develop their property quickly before a comprehensive plan can be enacted, thereby fostering inefficient and ill-conceived growth. . . .

Fairness Requires Informed Decision-Making in Land Use Planning

As Justice [Anthony] Kennedy explained in his opinion for the Court in *Palazzolo*, it is the interest in informed decision-making that underlies our decisions imposing a strict ripeness requirement on landowners asserting regulatory takings claims. . . .

We would create a perverse system of incentives were we to hold that landowners must wait for a taking claim to ripen so that planners can make well-reasoned decisions while, at the same time, holding that those planners must compensate landowners for the delay.

Indeed, the interest in protecting the decisional process is even stronger when an agency is developing a regional plan than when it is considering a permit for a single parcel. In the proceedings involving the Lake Tahoe Basin, for example, the moratoria enabled TRPA [Tahoe Regional Planning Agency] to obtain the benefit of comments and criticisms from interested parties, such as the petitioners, during its deliberations. Since a categorical rule tied to the length of deliberations would likely create added pressure on decision makers to reach a quick resolution of land-use questions, it would only serve to disadvantage those landowners and interest groups who are not as organized or familiar with the planning process. Moreover, with a temporary ban on development there is a lesser risk that individual landowners will be "singled out" to bear a special burden that should be shared by the public as a whole. At least with a moratorium there is a clear "reciprocity of advantage," *Mahon*, because it protects the interests of all affected landowners against immediate construction that might be inconsistent with the provisions of the plan that is ultimately adopted. "While each of us is burdened somewhat by such restrictions, we, in turn, benefit greatly from the restrictions that are placed on others" [*Keystone Bituminous Coal Assn. v. DeBenedictis* (1987)]. In fact, there is reason to believe property values often will continue to increase despite a moratorium. Such an increase makes sense in this context because property values throughout the [Lake Tahoe] Basin can be expected to reflect the added assurance that Lake Tahoe will remain in its pristine state. Since in some cases a one-year moratorium may not impose a burden at all, we should not adopt a rule that assumes moratoria always force individuals to bear a special burden that should be shared by the public as a whole.

It may well be true that any moratorium that lasts for more than one year should be viewed with special skepticism. But given the fact that the District Court found that the thirty months required by TRPA to formulate the 1984 Regional Plan was not unreasonable, we could not possibly conclude that every delay of over one year is constitutionally unacceptable. Formulating a general rule of this kind is a suitable task for state legislatures. In our view, the duration of the restriction is one of the important factors that a court must consider in the appraisal of a regulatory takings claim, but with respect to that factor as with respect to other factors, the "temptation to adopt what amount to *per se* rules in either direction must be resisted" (*Palazzolo*). There may be moratoria that last longer than one year which interfere with reasonable investment-backed expectations, but as the District Court's opinion illustrates, petitioners' proposed rule is simply "too blunt an instrument," for identifying those cases. We conclude, therefore, that the interest in "fairness and justice" will be best served by relying on the familiar *Penn Central* approach when deciding cases like this, rather than by attempting to craft a new categorical rule.

"As is the case with most governmental action that furthers the public interest, the Constitution requires that the costs and burdens be borne by the public at large, not by a few targeted citizens."

Dissenting Opinion: The Cost of Environmental Protection Should Be Borne by the Public at Large

William Rehnquist

William Rehnquist became a justice of the U.S. Supreme Court in 1972, and in 1986, he became chief justice, a position he held until his death in 2005. He was a strong conservative who believed in a strict interpretation of the Constitution. The following is his dissenting opinion in Tahoe-Sierra Preservation Council v. Tahoe Regional Planning Agency, *in which he argues that a ban on all property development for six years requires that the landowners be compensated. The precedent established in the* Lucas *case should have been followed, he says, because there is no good reason to distinguish between permanent loss of property and allegedly temporary loss when all a government agency would have to do is label a restriction on land use "temporary." He states that there was no need for the Court to worry about interfering with normal delays such as those involved in obtaining building permits, as these are traditionally expected, whereas a long-term moratorium is not normal. Chief Justice Rehnquist agrees that preserving Lake Tahoe is in the public interest, but*

William Rehnquist, dissenting opinion, *Tahoe-Sierra Preservation Council v. Tahoe Regional Planning Agency*, U.S. Supreme Court, April 23, 2002.

maintains that the cost of doing so should be borne by the public and not by a few targeted citizens.

For over half a decade petitioners were prohibited from building homes, or any other structures, on their land. Because the Takings Clause requires the government to pay compensation when it deprives owners of all economically viable use of their land [*Lucas v. South Carolina Coastal Council* (1992)] and because a ban on all development lasting almost six years does not resemble any traditional land-use planning device, I dissent.

"A court cannot determine whether a regulation has gone 'too far' unless it knows how far the regulation goes" [*MacDonald, Sommer & Eratee v. Yolo County* (1986) citing *Pennsylvania Coal Co. v. Mahon* (1922)]. In failing to undertake this inquiry, the Court ignores much of the impact of respondent's conduct on petitioners. Instead, it relies on the flawed determination of the Court of Appeals that the relevant time period lasted only from August 1981 until April 1984. During that period, Ordinance 81-5 and Regulation 83-21 prohibited development pending the adoption of a new regional land-use plan. The adoption of the 1984 Regional Plan (hereinafter Plan or 1984 Plan) did not, however, change anything from the petitioners' standpoint. After the adoption of the 1984 Plan, petitioners still could make no use of their land.

The Court of Appeals disregarded this post-April 1984 deprivation on the ground that respondent did not "cause" it. ... The Court of Appeals held that the 1984 Regional Plan did not amount to a taking because the Plan actually allowed permits to issue for the construction of single-family residences. Those permits were never issued because the District Court immediately issued a temporary restraining order, and later a permanent injunction that lasted until 1987, prohibiting the approval of any building projects under the 1984 Plan. Thus, the Court of Appeals concluded that the "1984 Plan itself could not have constituted a taking," because it was the injunction, not the Plan, that prohibited development during this period. The Court of Appeals is correct that the 1984 Plan did not cause petitioners' injury. But that is the right answer to the wrong question. The causation question is not limited to whether the 1984 Plan caused petitioners' injury; the question is whether respondent caused petitioners' injury.

We have never addressed §1983 causation requirement in the context of a regulatory takings claim ... The causation standard does not require much elaboration in this case, because respondent was undoubtedly the "moving force" behind petitioners' inability to build on their land from August 1984 through 1987. The injunction in this case issued because the 1984 Plan did not comply with the 1980 Tahoe Regional Planning Compact (Compact) and regulations issued pursuant to the Compact. . . .

Respondent is surely responsible for its own regulations, and it is also responsible for the Compact as it is the governmental agency charged with administering the Compact. It follows that respondent was the "moving force" behind petitioners' inability to develop its land from April 1984 through the enactment of the 1987 plan. Without the environmental thresholds established by the Compact and Resolution 82-11, the 1984 Plan would have gone into effect and petitioners would have been able to build single-family residences. And it was certainly foreseeable that development projects exceeding the environmental thresholds would be prohibited; indeed, that was the very purpose of enacting the thresholds.

Because respondent caused petitioners' inability to use their land from 1981 through 1987, that is the appropriate period of time from which to consider their takings claim.

The Temporary Denial of Land Use Is a Taking

I now turn to determining whether a ban on all economic development lasting almost six years is a taking. *Lucas* reaffirmed our "frequently expressed" view that "when the owner of real property has been called upon to sacrifice *all* economically beneficial uses in name of the common good, that is, to leave his property economically idle, he has suffered a taking." . . . But the Court refuses to apply *Lucas* on the ground that the deprivation was "temporary."

Neither the Takings Clause nor our case law supports such a distinction. For one thing, a distinction between "temporary" and "permanent" prohibitions is tenuous. The "temporary" prohibition in this case that the Court finds is not a taking lasted almost six years. The "permanent" prohibition that the Court held to be a taking in *Lucas* lasted less than two years. . . . Under the Court's decision today, the takings question turns entirely on the initial label given a regulation, a label that is often without much meaning. There is every incentive for government to simply label any prohibition on development "temporary," or to fix a set number of years. As in this case, this initial designation does not preclude the government from repeatedly extending the "temporary" prohibition into a long-term ban on all development. The Court now holds that such a designation by the government is conclusive even though in fact the moratorium greatly exceeds the time initially specified. Apparently, the Court would not view even a 10-year moratorium as a taking under *Lucas* because the moratorium is not "permanent." . . .

More fundamentally, even if a practical distinction between temporary and permanent deprivations were plausible, to treat the two differently in terms of takings law would be at odds with the justification for the *Lucas* rule. The *Lucas* rule is derived from the fact that a "total deprivation of use is, from the landowner's point of view, the equivalent of a physical appropriation." The regulation in *Lucas* was the "practical equivalence" of a long-term physical appropriation, *i.e.*, a condemnation, so the Fifth Amendment required compensation. The "practical equivalence," from the landowner's point of view, of a "temporary" ban on all economic use is a forced leasehold. For example, assume the following situation: Respondent is contemplating the creation of a National Park around Lake Tahoe to preserve its scenic beauty. Respondent decides to take a 6-year leasehold over petitioners' property, during which any human activity on the land would be prohibited, in order to prevent any further destruction to the area while it was deciding whether to request that the area be designated a National Park.

Surely that leasehold would require compensation. In a series of World War II-era cases in which the government had condemned leasehold interests in order to support the war effort, the government conceded that it was required to pay compensation for the leasehold interest. From petitioners' standpoint, what happened in this case is no different than if the government had taken a 6-year lease of their property. The Court ignores this "practical equivalence" between respondent's deprivation and the deprivation resulting from a leasehold. In so doing, the Court allows the government to "do by regulation what it cannot do through eminent domain—i.e., take private property without paying for it."

Instead of acknowledging the "practical equivalence" of this case and a condemned leasehold, the Court analogizes to other areas of takings law in which we have distinguished between regulations and physical appropriations. But whatever basis there is for such distinctions in those contexts does not apply when a regulation deprives a landowner of all economically beneficial use of his land. In addition to the "practical equivalence" from the landowner's perspective of such a regulation and a physical appropriation, we have held that a regulation denying all productive use of land does not implicate the traditional justification for differentiating between regulations and physical appropriations. In "the extraordinary circumstance when *no* productive or economically beneficial use of land is permitted," it is less likely that "the legislature is simply adjusting the benefits and burdens of economic life' in a manner that secures an 'average reciprocity of advantage' to everyone concerned," [*Lucas* quoting *Penn Central Transportation Co. v. New York City* (1978), and *Pennsylvania Coal Co. v. Mahon* (1922)] and more likely that the property "is being pressed into some form of public service under the guise of mitigating serious public harm." . . .

Because the rationale for the *Lucas* rule applies just as strongly in this case, the "temporary" denial of all viable use of land for six years is a taking.

Normal Delays Involved in Land Use Are Not Takings

The Court worries that applying *Lucas* here compels finding that an array of traditional, short-term, land-use planning devices are takings. But since the beginning of our regulatory takings jurisprudence, we have recognized that property rights "are enjoyed under an implied limitation" (*Pennsylvania Coal Co. v. Mahon*). Thus, in *Lucas*, after holding that the regulation prohibiting all economically beneficial use of the coastal land came within our categorical takings rule, we nonetheless inquired into whether such a result "inhere[d] in the title itself, in the restrictions that background principles of the State's law of property and nuisance already place upon land ownership." Because the regulation at issue in *Lucas* purported to be permanent, or at least long term, we concluded that the only implied limitation of state property law that could achieve a similar long-term deprivation of all economic use would be something "achieved in the courts—by adjacent landowners (or other uniquely affected persons) under the State's law of private nuisance, or by the State under its complementary power to abate nuisances that affect the public generally, or otherwise."

When a regulation merely delays a final land use decision, we have recognized that there are other background principles of state property law that prevent the delay from being deemed a taking. We thus noted in *First English* that our discussion of temporary takings did not apply "in the case of normal delays in obtaining building permits, changes in zoning ordinances, variances, and the like." We reiterated this last Term: "The right to improve property, of course, is subject to the reasonable exercise of state authority, including the enforcement of valid zoning and land-use restrictions" [*Palazzolo v. Rhode Island* (2001)]. . . . Thus, the short-term delays attendant to zoning and permit regimes are a long-standing feature of state property law and part of a landowner's reasonable investment-backed expectations.

But a moratorium prohibiting all economic use for a period of six years is not one of the long-standing, implied limitations of state property law. [According to E. Ziegler] moratoria are "interim controls on the use of land that seek to maintain the status quo with respect to land development in an area by either 'freezing' existing land uses or by allowing the issuance of building permits for only certain land uses that would not be inconsistent with a contemplated zoning plan or zoning change." Typical moratoria thus prohibit only certain categories of development, such as fast-food restaurants, or adult businesses, or all commercial development. Such moratoria do not implicate *Lucas* because they do not deprive landowners of all economically beneficial use of their land. . . . Moreover, unlike a permit system in which it is expected that a project will be approved so long as certain conditions are satisfied, a moratorium that prohibits all uses is by definition contemplating a new land-use plan that would prohibit all uses.

But this case does not require us to decide as a categorical matter whether moratoria prohibiting all economic use are an implied limitation of state property law, because the duration of this "moratorium" far exceeds that of ordinary moratoria. As the Court recognizes, state statutes authorizing the issuance of moratoria often limit the moratoria's duration. . . . Indeed, it has long been understood that moratoria on development exceeding these short time periods are not a legitimate planning device.

Resolution 83-21 reflected this understanding of the limited duration of moratoria in initially limiting the moratorium in this case to 90 days. But what resulted—a "moratorium" lasting nearly six years—bears no resemblance to the short-term nature of traditional moratoria as understood from these background examples of state property law.

Because the prohibition on development of nearly six years in this case cannot be said to resemble any "implied limitation" of state property law, it is a taking that requires compensation.

Lake Tahoe is a national treasure and I do not doubt that respondent's efforts at preventing further degradation of the lake were made in good faith in furtherance of the public interest. But, as is the case with most governmental action that furthers the public interest, the Constitution requires that the costs and burdens be borne by the public at large, not by a few targeted citizens. Justice Holmes' admonition of 80 years ago again rings true: "We arc in danger of forgetting that a strong public desire to improve the public condition is not enough to warrant achieving the desire by a shorter cut than the constitutional way of paying for the change."

"From landowners' perspective, a 'temporary' ban on land use is permanent—if it outlives them."

Temporary Moratoriums on Land Use Are Likely to Become Permanent

Harold Johnson

Harold Johnson is a staff attorney at the Pacific Legal Foundation, a Sacramento-based public-interest law firm that litigates for property rights and limited government, which submitted an amicus curiae (friend of the Court) brief in the Lake Tahoe case. In the following viewpoint, written prior to the Court's decision in Tahoe-Sierra Preservation Council v. Tahoe Regional Planning Agency, *Johnson argues that the government should not be allowed to avoid paying for land on which it has placed use restrictions because calling a ban on building "temporary" does not mean it will not last long enough to totally deprive owners of their property. He maintains that successive temporary bans are in effect permanent bans. Some people who have bought property near Lake Tahoe for retirement homes may not live long enough to use it, and even if they do, the delay will have permanently affected their lives. In Johnson's opinion, this is not fair; landowners who cannot build on their land should be paid for it.*

"But at my back I always hear Time's winged chariot hurrying near." Poet Andrew Marvell's reminder that life is short has special poignancy when you consider the hundreds of owners of small parcels near Lake Tahoe, who have grown old waiting for permission to build retirement or vacation homes on their land.

In early January, the Supreme Court heard a lawsuit brought by these landowners. The lawsuit challenges a construction ban in the Tahoe area that was imposed in 1981 and continues to this day—and yet still is labeled, in fine Orwellian parlance, a "temporary moratorium."

The Fifth Amendment says government must give owners "just compensation" when it takes private property. But the Tahoe landowners haven't been paid a dime. The question before the court: Can government evade the duty to pay by telling landowners that their property rights merely are being frozen for the time being—and they might get them back, someday, if they're lucky enough still to be alive?

Technically, the Supreme Court is reviewing only a three-year building moratorium decreed in the early 1980s by the Tahoe Regional Planning Agency, a growth-management authority set up by the states of California and Nevada. But the prohibition that ended in 1984 was followed immediately by another and then another.

Landowners Have Been Harmed by "Temporary" Loss of Property Rights

Back-to-back moratoria have forced landowners to watch grass grow on their empty lots for a generation. The owners retain title, pay taxes and face legal liability should anyone be injured on their property. But that's where their "rights" stop. Instead of getting restitution, they're forced into the role of unpaid conservators for land that the government has effectively designated as open space.

This isn't what Dorothy Cook had in mind when she bought a 60-x-100-foot Tahoe parcel in 1979 for $5,500. In her late 70s now, she shares a rented home with her sister and daughter in Big Bear City, Calif. She can't afford a house. Her only property is her tract near Tahoe, where she once dreamed of building a home for her golden years. "But the moratorium took away any possibility that I would ever have a home of my own for my retirement," she recently told the Medill News Service.

Medill also reported on Kenneth and Betty Eberle, who bought two wooded, adjoining lots in 1977 for $8,500 and $9,500, respectively. The Eberles were in their 40s at the time, with plans to save enough money to build a home for the day that they could retire. They even factored in the cost of hiring a soil engineer to make sure the project respected the natural beauty that drew them to the place and didn't harm the ecology. But dreams dimmed with the coming of the building moratorium and the signs it might last till the Twelfth of Never. One realtor recently told them the lots together would be worth $350,000 if there were permission to build. But while the "temporary" ban stays in place, the land is worthless, according to another realtor who recently appraised it.

"I basically had to agree with her," Kenneth Eberle said of that second, somber assessment. "I've been making tax payments for the last 24 years, and have not had any use of it."

The Eberles, Cook and more than 400 other landowners launched their legal challenges to the moratorium in the mid-1980s. They endured a long and costly procedural gauntlet before a federal district court finally held a bench trial on their case in 1998 and handed them a victory.

The judge found that they should indeed be paid for having lost the use of their property for three years, from 1981 through 1984. The decision relied on *Lucas v. South Carolina Coastal Council*, the landmark 1992 case in which the Supreme Court said that where a regulation denies all use and enjoyment of property, a "taking" has occurred and government must pay.

Lucas recognized that property doesn't have to be seized to be "taken." If officials prohibit you from doing anything on your land, you've been deprived of its productive use as effectively as if it had been condemned so a school or firehouse could be built. As the Supreme Court put it, "total deprivation of beneficial use is, from the landowner's point of view, the equivalent of a physical appropriation."

The Court of Appeals' Decision Was Wrong

The Tahoe plaintiffs hadn't savored their triumph more than one year before it was taken away by a three-judge panel of the 9th U.S. Circuit Court of Appeals. Judge Stephen Reinhardt, who wrote the appellate opinion, seemed to draw on medieval metaphysics in explaining why there should be no money for Cook and the others.

Property is more than square footage, Reinhardt asserted; property also has longevity—a life span that stretches beyond the horizon. If a regulation has a fixed ending, it hasn't robbed the owner of the property's full "temporal dimension" because there's some future point at which its use will be regained.

By this way of thinking, a three-year ban on development—or even a 24-year ban—doesn't raise constitutional problems, or at least is not a clear-cut taking. Even if it prevents the owner from using the property, it does so for only a fraction of the property's "temporal dimension," which conceivably extends from the Ice Age to the end of time.

Viewed from this eccentric perspective, even a "permanent" regulation could not be said to constitute a *per se* taking because no laws last forever—they're all temporary in the big picture. Reinhardt's approach also would give a pass to temporary physical invasions of property. What if government insisted on building a temporary road across your property to service a nearby highway project? Because the intrusion would have a conclusion, the Reinhardt rule implies you shouldn't be reimbursed for the time you were unable to use the property.

The ruling also runs afoul of legal precedent. Surely one reason the U.S. Supreme Court took the case is that it already has spoken on temporary takings—and the 9th Circuit did not seem to listen. The 1993 case, *First English Evangelical Lutheran Church vs. County of Los Angeles*, dealt with a county-development moratorium imposed after a flood in the Angeles National Forest. California courts said the moratorium should not be viewed as a taking if the county made it temporary by repealing it.

The U.S. Supreme Court held otherwise: "[W]here the government's activities have already worked a taking of all use of property, no subsequent action by the government can relieve it of the duty to provide compensation for the period during which the taking was effective." In other words, even a temporary prohibition triggers the Fifth Amendment duty to pay.

Ninth Circuit Judge Alex Kozinski, known for wry wit as well as commitment to property rights, notes that the three-judge panel in Tahoe seemed determined not to follow the Supreme Court's guidance: "The panel does not like the Supreme Court's takings-clause jurisprudence very much, so it reverses *First English*," Kozinski wrote in an opinion arguing for reconsideration of the *Tahoe* ruling.

The Supreme Court Should Reverse the Lower Court's Ruling

Now it's up to the Supreme Court to defend its precedents and reverse Judge Reinhardt (who's already perhaps the most reversed judge in the federal appellate system). Will the court do so? At oral argument, the landowners' lawyer came in for aggressive questioning, even from some of the more conservative judges, particularly on the implications of his position for run-of-the-mill land-use decisions.

Justices Sandra Day O'Connor and Anthony Kennedy, for instance, wondered whether delays in zoning decisions could be classified as temporary takings. The quite reasonable response: Zoning deliberations are fundamentally different from a construction moratorium. The former advance the development process while the latter slams on the brakes.

Many states give regulators no more than 60 days to review projects; it is disingenuous to compare these brief normal delays in the planning process with a multi-year freeze that brings the entire process to a halt.

Justice Antonin Scalia offered a reminder of the underlying purpose of the Fifth Amendment's takings clause: to ensure that the cost of important social purposes is shared broadly and not foisted onto a few people merely because they own property.

The Tahoe moratorium aims at keeping the lake pristine. "This is a general social problem for which the entire society should pay," Scalia said. If the landowners aren't paid for having their property taken out of commission, they bear the cost alone.

The justices should consider the message that bureaucrats might get if the 9th Circuit's ruling stands. If land use can be banned without worry, as long as the ban is "temporary," won't planners simply cobble together a chain of moratoria—as already has happened in Tahoe?

The matter of mortality also is worth a thought. From landowners' perspective, a "temporary" ban on land use is permanent—if it outlives them. Many of the Tahoe plaintiffs already are too old to take advantage of property they bought in the summer of life, when the first moratorium was not yet a twinkle in a regulator's eye. For these owners, the land-use freeze could be lifted tomorrow, but it still would have had a permanently damaging effect on their lives. If the Fifth Amendment has meaning, these people must be paid.

"With all the focus on alleged takings, we too often neglect the 'givings' side of the equation that shows how property owners benefit from land-use controls."

Temporary Moratoriums on Land Use Are Essential to Community Planning

Timothy J. Dowling

Timothy J. Dowling is chief counsel of the Community Rights Counsel, a nonprofit law firm that filed an amicus curiae (friend of the Court) brief in the Lake Tahoe case on behalf of the nation's governors, mayors, and county supervisors. In the following viewpoint, written prior to the Court's decision in Tahoe-Sierra Preservation Council v. Tahoe Regional Planning Agency, *he argues that property owners benefit from land-use planning and that it requires moratoria on building if it is to be done wisely instead of hurriedly. To demand compensation to landowners for every moratorium would, he says, take power from local authorities and give it to politically unaccountable federal judges. Moreover, Dowling states, most of the Lake Tahoe landowners did not suffer any loss, but sold their land for more than its purchase price. If there had been no moratorium and the beauty of Lake Tahoe had been destroyed by environmental*

Timothy J. Dowling, "Symposium—Does a Temporary Moratorium on Construction Constitute a Taking? No: It Is Essential to Sound Land-Use Planning That Protects Our Communities," *Insight on the News* (now owned by *Washington Times*), February 11, 2002.

damage, their land would have become worthless. To insist on compensation for every land restriction would, in his opinion, underline the very rights that property-rights groups aim to protect.

Reading the "takings" clause of the U.S. Constitution to require compensation for every temporary moratorium would violate the Constitution's plain text and original meaning, undermine important principles of federalism, and undercut the very property rights that supporters of the idea purport to cherish.

The Lake Tahoe moratorium case pending before the Supreme Court brings these issues into specific relief. Before turning to the Tahoe case, however, it is helpful to understand why moratoria are so essential.

Reasonable people welcome efforts by local planners and elected officials to keep adult bookstores and other unsavory enterprises away from our homes, to exclude polluting facilities such as corporate hog farms from our neighborhoods and to ensure that new communities have adequate schools, roads and sewers.

The basic question raised by temporary moratoria is whether we want land-use planning to be thoughtful and well-informed or rushed and irrational.

Good planning takes time, but planning efforts often trigger a race to the permit-application office by developers hoping to get their plans filed before new land-use controls kick in. Absent moratoria, new development would undermine planning measures before they even see the light of day. In the words of one court, without temporary moratoria, planning would "be like locking the stable after the horse is stolen."

Moratoria facilitate not only routine planning, but also efforts to address threats to public health and safety. Local officials have used moratoria to prohibit development on unstable slopes pending the adoption of construction guidelines.

In the landmark case of *First English Evangelical Lutheran Church v. County of Los Angeles* (1987), the county imposed a moratorium after a flash flood drowned 10 people and caused millions of dollars in property damage. The state courts ultimately ruled that the delay was not a taking, in large measure due to the underlying public-safety concerns.

May local officials impose moratoria without regard to fairness? Of course not. Courts use the due-process clause and other legal doctrines to ensure that moratoria are reasonable in scope and duration and imposed in good faith.

But reading the takings clause to require compensation for every moratorium, no matter how reasonable, would constitute blatant judicial activism. The Constitution's plain text requires compensation only where property is "taken," a term that suggests physical appropriation of land and does not readily embrace mere land-use regulation. Justice Antonin Scalia, writing for the Supreme Court in 1992, reminded us that for the first 150 years of our nation's history, courts applied the takings clause only to appropriations and physical invasions of property.

To be sure, in a seminal ruling of *Pennsylvania Coal Co. v. Mahon* (1922), the Supreme Court ruled that in extreme situations, land-use controls also may work a taking. But with due fidelity to the text and original understanding of the Constitution, the Supreme Court has made clear that regulation is a taking only in the rare case where the economic harm is so severe that it constitutes the functional equivalent of a physical appropriation. Most moratoria come nowhere close to this high standard. No court in the country has held that every temporary moratorium is a taking.

An activist application of the takings clause to every moratorium severely would undermine federalism. Land-use planning is quintessentially local in nature. Local officials are best positioned to address land-use issues and are most politically responsive to all affected landowners. Having federal judges look over the shoulders of local planners, city councils and county boards—threatening to impose financially ruinous compensation awards for every moratorium—would cause a huge power shift over land-use issues away from local officials to unelected, politically unaccountable, federal judges. Yet, in effect this is precisely the position advanced by the landowners in the Tahoe moratorium case.

Preserving Lake Tahoe's Beauty Protects Landowners

Lake Tahoe is the world's largest Alpine lake, covering more than 192 square miles. Surrounded by the snow-capped peaks of the Sierra Nevada mountains, the lake is world-renowned for its remarkable clarity. Mark Twain wrote that, in 80 feet of water, "every little pebble was distinct, every speckled trout, every hand's-breadth of sand. . . . The water was not merely transparent, but dazzlingly, brilliantly so." He concluded that "with the shadows of the mountains brilliantly photographed upon its still surface . . . it must be the fairest picture the whole earth affords." Lake Tahoe indisputably is a national treasure.

The lake's beauty and popularity, however, contain the seeds of its own destruction, for increased development in the Tahoe Basin slowly is ruining the lake. Homes, roads, parking lots and other impervious surfaces cover sensitive lands that previously absorbed rain and snowmelt. The increased runoff contains pollutants that spur the growth of algae, and the lake now is losing one foot of clarity each year. If development were uncontrolled, the lake's cobalt-blue waters would turn green and opaque for all eternity.

With the blessing of Congress, Nevada and California created the Tahoe Regional Planning Agency and directed it to establish a regional-development plan to protect the lake. The agency imposed a 32-month moratorium, from 1981 to 1984, to preserve the status quo on environmentally sensitive land while it prepared the regional plan. The trial court found that, given the scientific complexities involved, the 32-month moratorium was a reasonable, proportional and good-faith effort to protect the lake pending completion of the plan.

The federal appeals court that heard the case ruled that such moratoria do not constitute a taking because they preserve future development, which translates into substantial present value for affected landowners. The appellate court concluded that "given the importance and long-standing use of temporary moratoria, courts should be exceedingly reluctant to adopt rulings that would threaten the survival of this crucial planning mechanism."

Most Tahoe Landowners Suffered No Harm

The planning agency, the state and local government communities, and others who support the agency have argued before the U.S. Supreme Court that although compensation is warranted where moratoria truly are confiscatory or a mere sham to disguise permanent restrictions, reasonable moratoria are not takings. This position is consistent with common sense and decades of virtually unanimous legal precedent.

In contrast, the Tahoe landowners and so-called property-rights groups argue that every moratorium is a taking, no matter how reasonable in scope and duration, no matter how slight the impact on the landowner, and no matter how important the underlying government purpose. Under this reading, compensation in the form of fair rental value would be due even where the landowner was completely unaware of the moratorium or otherwise suffered no harm. For example, in the Tahoe case the trial court found that the average holding period for property in the Tahoe Basin is 20 years; a 32-month moratorium would not upset the expectations of most landowners. Not surprisingly, the Supreme Court justices gave the landowners' position a chilly reception at the Jan. 7 [2002] argument in the case.

The landowners assert that the 1987 *First English* ruling requires compensation for temporary moratoria. But *First English* holds only that compensation is required for a taking, and it expressly left unaddressed when land-use regulation works amount to a taking. The landowners also contend that compensation is due under a case called *Lucas v. South Carolina Coastal Council* (1992), but that ruling is limited to situations in which land is rendered valueless. The Tahoe landowners failed to introduce a shred of evidence that the 32-month moratorium reduced the value of their land, much less rendered it worthless. As is often the case in high-profile takings disputes, the so-called property-rights movement has tried to skew the debate by bending the truth, suggesting that none of the Tahoe claimants can build on their land even today. In fact, most of these landowners sold their property for more than their purchase price, and most of the rest now may build on their land.

The Supreme Court has made clear that the only issue before it in the Tahoe case is whether the 32-month moratorium worked a compensable taking. The irony, of course, is that if the planning agency had done nothing, all landowners would have suffered. How much would any land in the Tahoe Basin be worth if the lake were to turn green? With all the focus on alleged takings, we too often neglect the "givings" side of the equation that shows how property owners benefit from land-use controls that apply to their neighbors and the public at large.

Because the landowners' position is so extreme, the case has potential ramifications that extend far beyond Lake Tahoe. Consider the implications for national security. After the tragic events of Sept. 11 [,2001 terrorist attacks], the federal government ordered the temporary closure of Reagan National Airport and certain private airports in the Washington area to allow for careful re-evaluation of air-security concerns. If temporary denials of land use were takings, compensation claims could hinder reasonable efforts to respond to terrorists or otherwise enhance homeland security. Indeed, Justice Anthony Kennedy asked counsel for the Tahoe landowners whether, under their reading of the takings clause, compensation would be due if New York City were to impose a one-year delay on rebuilding the World Trade Center site. Such a delay might help the city study and address ongoing security concerns. Understandably, the landowners' attorney equivocated and then changed the subject. . . .

For the sake of truth in advertising, those who seek to undermine moratoria and other legitimate planning techniques should stop calling themselves property-rights advocates. The overwhelming majority of landowners in the United States are homeowners who derive tremendous benefits and significantly enhanced property values from moratoria, zoning and other planning efforts. Unduly expansive readings of the takings clause undermine the property rights that so-called property-rights groups say they want to protect.

> *"Any local government can deprive individuals of the right to use their property merely by being smart enough to set a termination date to any development moratorium it imposes."*

The Court Ignored Its Responsibility to Protect Individual Rights

John C. Eastman

John C. Eastman is dean of the Chapman University School of Law in Orange, California. In the following viewpoint, he argues that the founders of the nation considered the right to acquire and develop property to be a fundamental human right, and that the Supreme Court's decision in Tahoe-Sierra Preservation Council v. Tahoe Regional Planning Agency *struck a severe blow to that right. By balancing the harm to affected property owners against the benefit to the public, he says, the Court defeated the purpose of the Fifth Amendment's takings clause, which was to prevent government from forcing a few people to bear costs that should be borne by the public as a whole. If the government had to pay for land affected by building restrictions, then the burden of those restrictions would fall on everyone— that is, it would be shared by the taxpayers—instead of just on those who lost the use of their property. In Eastman's opinion, the Court failed in its responsibility to protect individual rights.*

John C. Eastman, "The Vanishing Right to Property," *Claremont Institute*, May 22, 2002. www.claremont.org. Copyright © 2002–2006 The Claremont Institute. Reproduced by permission.

In one of the most famous *Federalist Papers*, Federalist 10, James Madison wrote that the first object of government was the protection of the diversity of the faculties of men, from which the rights of property originate. The right to acquire and protect property was considered to be one of the fundamental, inalienable natural rights of mankind, and it is recognized as such in most of the original state constitutions and nearly all of the subsequent state constitutions. Pennsylvania's Constitution of 1776 is fairly typical, recognizing "That all men are born equally free and independent, and have certain natural, inherent, and inalienable rights, amongst which are, the enjoying and defending life and liberty, acquiring, possessing and protecting property, and pursuing and obtaining happiness and safety."

Last week [April 2002], the Supreme Court dealt a severe blow to the fundamental right of property owners to possess and actually use the property for which they had labored in their own pursuit of happiness. Affirming a 9th Circuit ruling by Judge Stephen Reinhardt that upheld a complete ban on new development in the Lake Tahoe basin in California and Nevada that has lasted now more than 20 years, Justice John Paul Stevens, writing for the Court in *Tahoe-Sierra Preservation Council, Inc. v. Tahoe Regional Planning Agency*, held that the initial 3-year moratorium on development was not a categorical taking because it deprived property owners of the use of their property for only a fraction of the property's entire useful life. By that reasoning, any local government can deprive individuals of the right to use their property merely by being smart enough to set a termination date to any development moratorium it imposes for what it deems to be in the public interest. As a result, hundreds of people who purchased property near Lake Tahoe for vacation or retirement homes will forever be barred from using their property as they intended.

What is most stunning about the decision is how fundamentally at odds it is with two relatively recent Supreme Court decisions. In the 1992 case of *Lucas v. South Carolina Coastal Council*, the Court held that a regulation that deprives a property owner of all economically beneficial use of his property was a categorical taking, requiring the payment of just compensation. And in the 1987 case of *First English Evangelical Lutheran Church of Glendale v. County of Los Angeles*, the Supreme Court held that property owners were entitled to just compensation even for regulatory bans on development that were only temporary.

To be fair, Justice Stevens' opinion, and the lower court opinion by Judge Reinhardt, can be viewed as a logical extension of the Supreme Court's earlier, and never repudiated, decision in *Penn Central Transportation Co. v. City of New York* [(1978)], but that just serves to highlight the analytical difficulties with the *Penn Central* decision itself, and the continuing threat to property rights that it poses.

The Court's Reasoning Threatens Property Rights

At issue in *Penn Central* was a New York City ordinance designating Grand Central Station as an historical landmark and prohibiting any development in, around, or above the station that would alter its aesthetic appeal. When the Court began focusing on whether the ordinance causes a significant enough decline in value to warrant being treated as a regulatory taking, *Penn Central* argued that the proper denominator for the equation was the value of the air rights [the right to build a tall building] alone, conceptually severed from the rest of the parcel. The Court rejected that contention, holding that only significant declines in value to the parcel as a whole would be treated as regulatory takings.

There are two fundamental problems with the *Penn Central* analysis, particularly as extended by Justice Stevens in

Tahoe-Sierra. First, rejecting the doctrine of conceptual severance in the regulatory takings context ignores the fact that property rights themselves are often conceptually severed. A brief hypothetical example will highlight the problem. Suppose the New York ordinance also applied to St. Patrick's Cathedral, but the Archdioceses of New York had sold off the air space above the Cathedral for development prior to the enactment of the ordinance. The ordinance would amount to a categorical taking because it would deprive the Cathedral Development Corp. from all beneficial use, but it would not amount to a categorical taking from *Penn Central*, because the latter still retained the larger parcel from which the air rights had been severed in the former.

A similar hypothetical can demonstrate the fallacy of Justice Stevens' rejection of "temporal" conceptual severance. Imagine two adjoining vacant lots in Lake Tahoe, both purchased in 1980 shortly before the development moratorium was issued. Property owner A keeps the entire parcel himself, but property owner B sells a 3-year leasehold in the property to a developer, who will develop the property and then be paid for the additional value created at the end of the lease. A 3-year development moratorium would deprive B's lessee of all use, and thus be a categorical taking for which compensation must be paid, but without conceptual severance it would only deprive A of a portion of his use, and hence not be a compensable taking.

More fundamentally, by balancing the property owner's harms against the benefit to the public in determining whether a taking has even occurred, the *Penn Central* analysis simply repudiates the purpose of the takings clause. As Chief Justice Rehnquist wrote for the Court in *First English*, "[i]t is axiomatic that the Fifth Amendment's just compensation provision is 'designed to bar government from forcing some people alone to bear public burdens which, in all fairness and justice, should be borne by the public as a whole.'" Less development in Lake Tahoe undoubtedly will help preserve the pristine clarity of the Lake, certainly a public good. By requiring government to pay for the prohibition on development by some property owners, the entire public benefited by the prohibition would share in the cost (via increased property taxes for those who have already built their homes in the area and perhaps a hotel occupancy tax for those who merely visit). Without such a requirement, the entire cost of the public benefit is borne by the handful of property owners—certainly a good deal for existing homeowners, but hardly fair for those whose own life pursuit of happiness was regulated into nothingness for the benefit of others. There is a real danger of majority tyranny here, and the Court is simply abrogating its responsibility to protect individual rights as long as it continues to adhere to (and even expand) the pernicious *Penn Central* ruling.

CHAPTER 3

Cities May Condemn Homes to Make Way for Commercial Development

Case Overview

Kelo et al. v. City of New London et al. (2005)

Wilhelmina Dery had lived for eighty-two years in the Fort Trumbull, Connecticut, house in which she was born. Her husband Charles had lived there since their marriage, and their son lived next door in a house they had given him as a wedding present. So when the city of New London decided to condemn their homes and force them to move, they were not happy. Neither was Susette Kelo, who had made extensive improvements to her house—which she prized for its water view—or any of the seven other property owners who had refused to sell. None of the homes were in poor condition; they were condemned only because they happened to be located in an area where the city wanted to put a commercial development centered on a new research facility for the pharmaceutical company Pfizer.

Can a local government seize property against the will of its owners? Yes, it can; that has always been true. If the land is taken for public use, such as a highway or a municipal building, government has a right to take it; this is called the power of "eminent domain." The takings clause of the Constitution's Fifth Amendment states, however, that the owner must receive fair compensation, that is, an amount of money equal to the market value of the land. Susette Kelo and the other owners involved did not dispute the price they were offered. They took their case to court because of another restriction in the takings clause: public use. They maintained that commercial development is not public use, and that the city, therefore, could not legally condemn their homes.

The lower court held that under state law, taking land for an economic development project was defined as "public use" and in the public interest; but it issued a restraining order prohibiting the taking of the property before the issue was settled. The case then went to the Superior Court of Connecticut, which ruled that the city's proposed takings were legal. The Supreme Court agreed to review the decision in order to determine whether economic development satisfies the "public use" requirement of the Fifth Amendment.

This was an extremely controversial case, and the outcome shocked and outraged people throughout the nation. The Court ruled five–four that economic development is of benefit to the public and cannot be distinguished from other beneficial uses, as long as the land is not taken for the benefit of particular private parties. Urban planning involving coordination of different land uses has long been acceptable, it said, and because such plans serve a public purpose, they meet the Fifth Amendment's requirements. That, the Court stated, was all it had authority to decide, though states are free to place more restrictions on takings if they wish to do so.

The four dissenters were dismayed by this decision. Justice Clarence Thomas wrote, "The Court replaces the Public Use Clause [of the Fifth Amendment] with a 'Public Purpose' Clause, (or perhaps [quoting the majority opinion] the 'Diverse and Always Evolving Needs of Society' Clause), a restriction that is satisfied, the Court instructs, so long as the purpose is 'legitimate' and the means 'not irrational.' This deferential shift in phraseology enables the Court to hold, against all common sense, that a costly urban-renewal project whose stated purpose is a vague promise of new jobs and increased tax revenue, but which is also suspiciously agreeable to the Pfizer Corporation, is for a 'public use. . . .' The most natural reading of the [Takings] Clause is that it allows the government to take property only if the government owns, or the public has a legal right to use, the property, as opposed to taking it for any public purpose or necessity whatsoever."

That was what most people had assumed it meant. Though some commentators argued that the decision did not really add to the power government already possessed, the public had not been aware of the ways in which that power was being used. Therefore, the *Kelo* case caused a nationwide backlash against eminent domain abuse. On June 23, 2008, the third anniversary of the Supreme Court's ruling, Susette Kelo's house—which was moved to another location after the property was seized—was dedicated as a monument to the property-rights movement by the new owner who now lives in it. As of that date, the development for which the city of New London demolished the homes has yet to take place; the land on which those homes once stood remains barren. But there have been eminent domain reforms in forty-two states, some of which provide strong protections for property owners, and a number of bills with this aim have been introduced in Congress.

> "Nothing in our opinion precludes any
> State from placing further restrictions
> on its exercise of the takings power."

The Court's Decision: Economic Development Qualifies as Public Use Under the Fifth Amendment to the Constitution

John Paul Stevens

John Paul Stevens is, as of 2008, the oldest and longest-serving member of the Supreme Court and is generally considered to be the leader of its liberal faction. The following is his majority opinion in Kelo et al. v. City of New London et al., *a case in which private homes were condemned by the city to make room for a new commercial development. The homeowners were to be paid for their land, but they did not want to move and protested that forcing them to do so was a violation of the Fifth Amendment's taking clause, which allows government to take property only for public use. Justice Stevens explains in the Court's ruling that economic development is of benefit to the public and that, according to the precedents set by other cases, it cannot be distinguished from other public uses that have been considered allowable. States are free to place stricter limits on the power of government to take property, he says, but the Court has authority only to decide whether the taking in this case is permitted by the Constitution.*

John Paul Stevens, majority opinion, *Kelo et al. v. City of New London et al.*, U.S. Supreme Court, June 23, 2005.

Two polar propositions are perfectly clear. On the one hand, it has long been accepted that the sovereign may not take the property of A for the sole purpose of transferring it to another private party B, even though A is paid just compensation. On the other hand, it is equally clear that a State may transfer property from one private party to another if future "use by the public" is the purpose of the taking; the condemnation of land for a railroad with common-carrier duties is a familiar example. Neither of these propositions, however, determines the disposition of this case.

As for the first proposition, the City would no doubt be forbidden from taking petitioners' land for the purpose of conferring a private benefit on a particular private party. Nor would the City be allowed to take property under the mere pretext of a public purpose, when its actual purpose was to bestow a private benefit. The takings before us, however, would be executed pursuant to a "carefully considered" development plan. The trial judge and all the members of the Supreme Court of Connecticut agreed that there was no evidence of an illegitimate purpose in this case. Therefore ... the City's development plan was not adopted "to benefit a particular class of identifiable individuals."

On the other hand, this is not a case in which the City is planning to open the condemned land—at least not in its entirety—to use by the general public. Nor will the private lessees of the land in any sense be required to operate like common carriers, making their services available to all comers. But although such a projected use would be sufficient to satisfy the public use requirement, this "Court long ago rejected any literal requirement that condemned property be put into use for the general public" [*Hawaii Housing Authority v. Midkiff* (1984)]. Indeed, while many state courts in the mid-19th century endorsed "use by the public" as the proper definition of public use, that narrow view steadily eroded over time. Not only was the "use by the public" test difficult to administer (*e.g.*, what proportion of the public need have access to the property? at what price?), but it proved to be impractical given the diverse and always evolving needs of society. Accordingly, when this Court began applying the Fifth Amendment to the States at the close of the 19th century, it embraced the broader and more natural interpretation of public use as "public purpose." Thus, in a case upholding a mining company's use of an aerial bucket line to transport ore over property it did not own, Justice [Oliver Wendell] Holmes' opinion for the Court stressed "the inadequacy of use by the general public as a universal test" [*Strickley v. Highland Boy Gold Mining Co.* (1906)]. We have repeatedly and consistently rejected that narrow test ever since.

Does the City's Plan Serve a Public Purpose?

The disposition of this case therefore turns on the question whether the City's development plan serves a "public purpose." Without exception, our cases have defined that concept broadly, reflecting our longstanding policy of deference to legislative judgments in this field.

In *Berman v. Parker* (1954), this Court upheld a redevelopment plan targeting a blighted area of Washington, D. C., in which most of the housing for the area's 5,000 inhabitants was beyond repair. Under the plan, the area would be condemned and part of it utilized for the construction of streets, schools, and other public facilities. The remainder of the land would be leased or sold to private parties for the purpose of redevelopment, including the construction of low-cost housing.

The owner of a department store located in the area challenged the condemnation, pointing out that his store was not itself blighted and arguing that the creation of a "better balanced, more attractive community" was not a valid public use. Writing for a unanimous Court, Justice [William O.] Douglas refused to evaluate this claim in isolation, deferring instead to the legislative and agency judgment that the area "must be planned as a whole" for the plan to be successful. The Court explained that "community redevelopment programs need not, by force of the Constitution, be on a piecemeal basis—lot by lot, building by building." The public use underlying the taking was unequivocally affirmed:

> "We do not sit to determine whether a particular housing project is or is not desirable. The concept of the public welfare is broad and inclusive.... The values it represents are spiritual as well as physical, aesthetic as well as monetary. It is within the power of the legislature to determine that the community should be beautiful as well as healthy, spacious as well as clean, well-balanced as well as carefully patrolled. In the present case, the Congress and its authorized agencies have made determinations that take into account a wide variety of values. It is not for us to reappraise them. If those who govern the District of Columbia decide that the Nation's Capital should be beautiful as well as sanitary, there is nothing in the Fifth Amendment that stands in the way."

In *Hawaii Housing Authority v. Midkiff* (1954), the Court considered a Hawaii statute whereby fee title was taken from lessors and transferred to lessees (for just compensation) in order to reduce the concentration of land ownership. We unanimously upheld the statute and rejected the Ninth Circuit's view that it was "a naked attempt on the part of the state of Hawaii to take the property of *A* and transfer it to *B* solely for *B*'s private use and benefit." Reaffirming *Berman's* deferential approach to legislative judgments in this field, we concluded that the State's purpose of eliminating the "social and economic evils of a land oligopoly" qualified as a valid public use. Our opinion also rejected the contention that the mere fact that the State immediately transferred the properties to private individuals upon condemnation somehow diminished the public character of the taking. "[I]t is only the taking's purpose, and not its mechanics," we explained, that matters in determining public use....

Viewed as a whole, our jurisprudence has recognized that the needs of society have varied between different parts of the

Nation, just as they have evolved over time in response to changed circumstances. . . . For more than a century, our public use jurisprudence has wisely eschewed rigid formulas and intrusive scrutiny in favor of affording legislatures broad latitude in determining what public needs justify the use of the takings power.

Those who govern the City were not confronted with the need to remove blight in the Fort Trumbull area, but their determination that the area was sufficiently distressed to justify a program of economic rejuvenation is entitled to our deference. The City has carefully formulated an economic development plan that it believes will provide appreciable benefits to the community, including—but by no means limited to—new jobs and increased tax revenue. As with other exercises in urban planning and development, the City is endeavoring to coordinate a variety of commercial, residential, and recreational uses of land, with the hope that they will form a whole greater than the sum of its parts. To effectuate this plan, the City has invoked a state statute that specifically authorizes the use of eminent domain to promote economic development. Given the comprehensive character of the plan, the thorough deliberation that preceded its adoption, and the limited scope of our review, it is appropriate for us, as it was in *Berman*, to resolve the challenges of the individual owners, not on a piecemeal basis, but rather in light of the entire plan. Because that plan unquestionably serves a public purpose, the takings challenged here satisfy the public use requirement of the Fifth Amendment.

Economic Development Cannot Be Distinguished from Other Public Purposes

To avoid this result, petitioners urge us to adopt a new bright-line rule that economic development does not qualify as a public use. Putting aside the unpersuasive suggestion that the City's plan will provide only purely economic benefits, neither precedent nor logic supports petitioners' proposal. Promoting economic development is a traditional and long accepted function of government. There is, moreover, no principled way of distinguishing economic development from the other public purposes that we have recognized. . . .

Petitioners contend that using eminent domain for economic development impermissibly blurs the boundary between public and private takings. Again, our cases foreclose this objection. Quite simply, the government's pursuit of a public purpose will often benefit individual private parties. For example, in *Midkiff*, the forced transfer of property conferred a direct and significant benefit on those lessees who were previously unable to purchase their homes. . . . The owner of the department store in *Berman* objected to "taking from one businessman for the benefit of another businessman," referring to the fact that under the redevelopment plan land would be leased or sold to private developers for redevelopment. Our rejection of that contention has particular relevance to the instant case: "The public end may be as well or better served through an agency of private enterprise than through a department of government—or so the Congress might conclude. We cannot say that public ownership is the sole method of promoting the public purposes of community redevelopment projects."

It is further argued that without a bright-line rule nothing would stop a city from transferring citizen *A*'s property to citizen *B* for the sole reason that citizen *B* will put the property to a more productive use and thus pay more taxes. Such a one-to-one transfer of property, executed outside the confines of an integrated development plan, is not presented in this case. While such an unusual exercise of government power would certainly raise a suspicion that a private purpose was afoot, the hypothetical cases posited by petitioners can be confronted if and when they arise. They do not warrant the crafting of an artificial restriction on the concept of public use.

Alternatively, petitioners maintain that for takings of this kind we should require a "reasonable certainty" that the expected public benefits will actually accrue. Such a rule, however, would represent an even greater departure from our precedent. "When the legislature's purpose is legitimate and its means are not irrational, our cases make clear that empirical debates over the wisdom of takings—no less than debates over the wisdom of other kinds of socioeconomic legislation—are not to be carried out in the federal courts" (*Midkiff*). . . . A constitutional rule that required postponement of the judicial approval of every condemnation until the likelihood of success of the plan had been assured would unquestionably impose a significant impediment to the successful consummation of many such plans.

Just as we decline to second-guess the City's considered judgments about the efficacy of its development plan, we also decline to second-guess the City's determinations as to what lands it needs to acquire in order to effectuate the project. "It is not for the courts to oversee the choice of the boundary line nor to sit in review on the size of a particular project area. Once the question of the public purpose has been decided, the amount and character of land to be taken for the project and the need for a particular tract to complete the integrated plan rests in the discretion of the legislative branch" (*Berman*).

In affirming the City's authority to take petitioners' properties, we do not minimize the hardship that condemnations may entail, notwithstanding the payment of just compensation. We emphasize that nothing in our opinion precludes any State from placing further restrictions on its exercise of the takings power. Indeed, many States already impose "public use" requirements that are stricter than the federal baseline. Some of these requirements have been established as a matter of state constitutional law, while others are expressed in state eminent domain statutes that carefully limit the grounds upon which takings may be exercised. As the submissions of the parties and their *amici* make clear, the necessity and wisdom of using eminent domain to promote economic development are certainly matters of legitimate public debate. This Court's authority, however, extends only to determining whether the City's proposed condemnations are for a "public use" within the meaning of the Fifth Amendment to the Federal Constitution. Because over a century of our case law interpreting that provision dictates an affirmative answer to that question, we may not grant petitioners the relief that they seek.

> *"The specter of condemnation hangs over all property. Nothing is to prevent the State from replacing any Motel 6 with a Ritz-Carlton, any home with a shopping mall, or any farm with a factory."*

Dissenting Opinion: The Court's Decision Eliminates Any Distinction Between Private and Public Use of Property

Sandra Day O'Connor

Sandra Day O'Connor was the first woman justice of the Supreme Court, where she served from 1981 until her retirement in 2006. As a swing vote between its conservative and liberal factions, she was often extremely influential. The following is her dissenting opinion in Kelo et al. v. City of New London et al., *in which she argues that the Court's ruling eliminates the distinction between public and private property. She declares that economic development is not "public use" within the meaning of the Constitution. If it is legal for government to acquire property against the owner's will merely for economic development, she says, then any home or small business can be taken for the benefit of a large corporation. She maintains that through this ruling, the government has been given the power to transfer property from those with fewer resources to those with more, and believes this cannot be what the Founders intended.*

Sandra Day O'Connor, dissenting opinion, *Kelo et al. v. City of New London et al.*, U.S. Supreme Court, June 23, 2005.

Over two centuries ago, just after the Bill of Rights was ratified, Justice [Samuel] Chase wrote:

"An *act* of the Legislature (for I cannot call it a law) contrary to the great first principles of the social compact, cannot be considered a rightful exercise of legislative authority. . . . A few instances will suffice to explain what I mean. . . . [A] law that takes property from A and gives it to B: It is against all reason and justice, for a people to entrust a Legislature with *such* powers; and, therefore, it cannot be presumed that they have done it."

Today the Court abandons this long-held, basic limitation on government power. Under the banner of economic development, all private property is now vulnerable to being taken and transferred to another private owner, so long as it might be upgraded—*i.e.*, given to an owner who will use it in a way that the legislature deems more beneficial to the public—in the process. To reason, as the Court does, that the incidental public benefits resulting from the subsequent ordinary use of private property render economic development takings "for public use" is to wash out any distinction between private and public use of property—and thereby effectively to delete the words "for public use" from the Takings Clause of the Fifth Amendment. Accordingly I respectfully dissent.

Petitioners are nine resident or investment owners of fifteen homes in the Fort Trumbull neighborhood of New London, Connecticut. Petitioner Wilhelmina Dery, for example, lives in a house on Walbach Street that has been in her family for over 100 years. She was born in the house in 1918; her husband, petitioner Charles Dery, moved into the house when they married in 1946. Their son lives next door with his family in the house he received as a wedding gift, and joins his parents in this suit. . . .

To save their homes, petitioners sued New London and the NLDC [New London Development Corporation], to whom New London has delegated eminent domain [the power of government to take property] power. Petitioners maintain that the Fifth Amendment prohibits the NLDC from condemning their properties for the sake of an economic development plan. Petitioners are not hold-outs; they do not seek increased compensation, and none is opposed to new development in the area. Theirs is an objection in principle: They claim that the NLDC's proposed use for their confiscated property is not a "public" one for purposes of the Fifth Amendment. While the government may take their homes to build a road or a railroad or to eliminate a property use that harms the public, say petitioners, it cannot take their property for the private use of other owners simply because the new owners may make more productive use of the property.

The Constitution Limits the Taking of Property

The Fifth Amendment to the Constitution, made applicable to the States by the Fourteenth Amendment, provides that "private property [shall not] be taken for public use, without just compensation." When interpreting the Constitution, we begin with the unremarkable presumption that every word in the document has independent meaning, "that no word was unnecessarily used, or needlessly added" [*Wright v. United States* (1938)]. In keeping with that presumption, we have read the Fifth Amendment's language to impose two distinct conditions on the exercise of eminent domain: "The taking must be for a 'public use' and 'just compensation' must be paid to the owner" [*Brown v. Legal Foundation of Wash.* (2003)].

These two limitations serve to protect "the security of Property," which Alexander Hamilton described to the Philadelphia Convention as one of the "great obj[ects] of Gov[ernment]." Together they ensure stable property ownership by providing safeguards against excessive, unpredictable, or unfair use of the government's eminent domain power—particularly against those owners who, for whatever reasons, may be unable to protect themselves in the political process against the majority's will.

While the Takings Clause presupposes that government can take private property without the owner's consent, the just compensation requirement spreads the cost of condemnations and thus "prevents the public from loading upon one individual more than his just share of the burdens of government" [*Monongahela Nav. Co. v. United States* (1893)]. The public use requirement, in turn, imposes a more basic limitation, circumscribing the very scope of the eminent domain power: Government may compel an individual to forfeit her property for the *public's* use, but not for the benefit of another private person. This requirement promotes fairness as well as security.

Where is the line between "public" and "private" property use? We give considerable deference to legislatures' determinations about what governmental activities will advantage the public. But were the political branches the sole arbiters of the public-private distinction, the Public Use Clause would amount to little more than hortatory fluff. An external, judicial check on how the public use requirement is interpreted, however limited, is necessary if this constraint on government power is to retain any meaning.

Our cases have generally identified three categories of takings that comply with the public use requirement, though it is in the nature of things that the boundaries between these categories are not always firm. Two are relatively straightforward and uncontroversial. First, the sovereign may transfer private property to public ownership—such as for a road, a hospital, or a military base. Second, the sovereign may transfer private property to private parties, often common carriers, who make the property available for the public's use—such as with a railroad, a public utility, or a stadium. But "public ownership" and "use-by-the-public" are sometimes too constricting and impractical ways to define the scope of the Public Use Clause. Thus we have allowed that, in certain circumstances and to meet certain exigencies, takings that serve a public purpose also satisfy the Constitution even if the property is destined for subsequent private use.

Economic Development Takings Are Not Constitutional

This case returns us for the first time in over twenty years to the hard question of when a purportedly "public purpose" taking meets the public use requirement. It presents an issue of first impression: Are economic development takings constitutional? I would hold that they are not. We are guided by two precedents about the taking of real property by eminent domain. In *Berman* [*v. Parker* (1954)] we upheld takings within a blighted neighborhood of Washington, D.C. The neighborhood had so deteriorated that, for example, 64.3 percent of its dwellings were beyond repair. It had become burdened with "overcrowding of dwellings," "lack of adequate streets and alleys," and "lack of light and air." Congress had determined that the neighborhood had become "injurious to the public health, safety, morals, and welfare" and that it was necessary to "eliminat[e] all such injurious conditions by employing all means necessary and appropriate for the purpose," including eminent domain. Mr. Berman's department store was not itself blighted. Having approved of Congress's decision to eliminate the harm to the public emanating from the blighted neighborhood, however, we did not second-guess its decision to treat the neighborhood as a whole rather than lot-by-lot.

In [*Hawaii Housing Authority v.*] *Midkiff* [1984], we upheld a land condemnation scheme in Hawaii whereby title in real property was taken from lessors and transferred to lessees. . . .

In those decisions, we emphasized the importance of deferring to legislative judgments about public purpose. . . . Likewise, we recognized our inability to evaluate whether, in a given case, eminent domain is a necessary means by which to pursue the legislature's ends.

Yet for all the emphasis on deference, *Berman* and *Midkiff* hewed to a bedrock principle without which our public use jurisprudence would collapse: "A purely private taking could not withstand the scrutiny of the public use requirement; it would serve no legitimate purpose of government and would thus be void" (*Midkiff*). To protect that principle, those decisions reserved "a role for courts to play in reviewing a legislature's judgment of what constitutes a public use . . . [though] the Court in *Berman* made clear that it is 'an extremely narrow' one" (*Midkiff*, quoting *Berman*).

The Court's holdings in *Berman* and *Midkiff* were true to the principle underlying the Public Use Clause. In both those cases, the extraordinary, precondemnation use of the targeted property inflicted affirmative harm on society—in *Berman* through blight resulting from extreme poverty and in *Midkiff* through oligopoly resulting from extreme wealth. And in both cases, the relevant legislative body had found that eliminating the existing property use was necessary to remedy the harm. Thus a public purpose was realized when the harmful use was eliminated. Because each taking *directly* achieved a public benefit, it did not matter that the property was turned over to private use. Here, in contrast, New London does not claim that Susette Kelo's and Wilhelmina Dery's well-maintained homes are the source of any social harm. Indeed, it could not so claim without adopting the absurd argument that any single-family home that might be razed to make way for an apartment building, or any church that might be replaced with a retail store, or any small business that might be more lucrative if it were instead part of a national franchise, is inherently harmful to society and thus within the government's power to condemn.

In moving away from our decisions sanctioning the condemnation of harmful property use, the Court today significantly expands the meaning of public use. It holds that the sovereign may take private property currently put to ordinary private use, and give it over for new, ordinary private use, so long as the new use is predicted to generate some secondary benefit for the public—such as increased tax revenue, more jobs, maybe even aesthetic pleasure. But nearly any lawful use of real private property can be said to generate some incidental benefit to the public. Thus, if predicted (or even guaranteed) positive side-effects are enough to render transfer from one private party to another constitutional, then the words "for public use" do not realistically exclude *any* takings, and thus do not exert any constraint on the eminent domain power. . . .

The court protests that it does not sanction the bare transfer from A to B for B's benefit. It suggests two limitations on what can be taken after today's decision. First, it maintains a role for courts in ferreting out takings whose sole purpose is to bestow a benefit on the private transferee—without detailing how courts are to conduct that complicated inquiry. . . .

The Court's Ruling Means Any Property Can Now Be Taken

Even if there were a practical way to isolate the motives behind a given taking, the gesture toward a purpose test is theoretically flawed. If it is true that incidental public benefits from new private use are enough to ensure the "public purpose" in a taking, why should it matter, as far as the Fifth Amendment is concerned, what inspired the taking in the first place? How much the government does or does not desire to benefit a favored private party has no bearing on whether an economic development taking will or will not generate secondary benefit for the public. And whatever the reason for a given condemnation, the effect is the same from the constitutional perspective—private property is forcibly relinquished to new private ownership.

A second proposed limitation is implicit in the Court's opinion. The logic of today's decision is that eminent domain may only be used to upgrade—not downgrade—property. At best this makes the Public Use Clause redundant with the Due Process Clause, which already prohibits irrational government action. The Court rightfully admits, however, that the judiciary cannot get bogged down in predictive judgments about whether the public will actually be better off after a property transfer. In any event, this constraint has no realistic import. For who among us can say she already makes the most productive or attractive possible use of her property? The specter of condemnation hangs over all property. Nothing is to prevent the State from replacing any Motel 6 with a Ritz-Carlton, any home with a shopping mall, or any farm with a factory.

If legislative prognostications about the secondary public benefits of a new use can legitimate a taking, there is nothing in the Court's rule . . . to prohibit property transfers generated with less care, that are less comprehensive, that happen to result from less elaborate process, whose only projected advantage is the incidence of higher taxes, or that hope to transform an already prosperous city into an even more prosperous one.

Finally, in a coda, the Court suggests that property owners should turn to the States, who may or may not choose to impose appropriate limits on economic development takings. This is an abdication of our responsibility. States play many important functions in our system of dual sovereignty, but compensating for our refusal to enforce properly the Federal Constitution (and a provision meant to curtail state action, no less) is not among them.

It was possible after *Berman* and *Midkiff* to imagine unconstitutional transfers from *A* to *B*. Those decisions endorsed government intervention when private property use had veered to such an extreme that the public was suffering as a consequence. Today nearly all real property is susceptible to condemnation on the Court's theory. In the prescient words of a dissenter from the infamous decision in *Poletown* [*Neighborhood Council v. City of Detroit* (1981)], "[n]ow that we have authorized local legislative bodies to decide that a different commercial or industrial use of property will produce greater public benefits than its present use, no homeowner's, merchant's or manufacturer's property, however productive or valuable to its owner, is immune from condemnation for the benefit of other private interests that will put it to a 'higher' use." This is why economic development takings "seriously jeopardiz[e] the security of all private property ownership."

Any property may now be taken for the benefit of another private party, but the fallout from this decision will not be random. The beneficiaries are likely to be those citizens with disproportionate influence and power in the political process, including large corporations and development firms. As for the victims, the government now has license to transfer property from those with fewer resources to those with more. The Founders cannot have intended this perverse result. "[T]hat alone is a *just* government," wrote James Madison, "which *impartially* secures to every man, whatever is his *own*."

"After declaring that all property is subject to the whim of a government official, it's just a short trip to declaring that government can now confiscate anything we own."

The Taking of Private Property for Economic Development Amounts to Theft

Tom DeWeese

Tom DeWeese is the publisher/editor of The DeWeese Report *and president of the American Policy Center. In the following viewpoint, he declares that the government taking private property for commercial development amounts to theft, that the Supreme Court's decision allowing it puts all Americans in danger of losing their homes, and that it is contrary to the principles of the nation's founders. He is critical of the Supreme Court justices who voted for this decision in* Kelo et al. v. City of New London et al. *and declares that they ignored the Constitution in order to support the international policy of sustainable development. This policy, he says, has permitted corrupt politicians in some cities to partner with commercial developers and take property for personal gain in the name of the "public good." However, Americans have begun to fight back through state and local laws, and in DeWeese's opinion, they must work harder for passage of such laws.*

Tom DeWeese, "Organized Theft: Sustainable Development, Smart Growth, and *Kelo*," *Capitalism Magazine*, July 3, 2005. www.capmag.com. *Capitalism Magazine* Copyright © 2005 Bahamas 2005, Ltd. All rights reserved. Reproduced by permission.

Put yourself in the homeowner's shoes. You buy a home for your family. Perhaps it's even handed down from your father or grandfather. It's a place you can afford in a neighborhood you like. The children have made friends. You intend to stay for the rest of your life.

As you plant your garden, landscape the yard, put up a swing set for the kids, and mold your land into a home, unknown to you, certain city officials are meeting around a table with developers. In front of them are maps, plats and photographs—of your home. They talk of dollars—big dollars. Tax revenues for the city, huge profits for the developer. A shopping center with all the trimmings begins to take shape. You're not asked for input or permission. You're not even notified until the whole project is finalized and the only minor detail is to get rid of you.

Then the pressure begins. A notice comes in the mail telling you that the city intends to take your land. An offer of compensation is made, usually below the market price you could get if you sold it yourself. The explanation given is that, since the government is going to take the land, it's not worth the old market price. Some neighbors begin to sell and move away. With the loss of each one, the pressure mounts on you to sell. Visits from government agents become routine. Newspaper articles depict you as unreasonably holding up community progress. They call you greedy. Finally, the bulldozers move in on the properties already sold. The neighborhood becomes unlivable. It looks like a war zone.

Like being attacked by a conquering army, you are finally surrounded, with no place to run, but the courts. However, you're certain of victory. The United States was built on the very premise of the protection of private property rights. How can a government possibly be allowed to take anyone's home for private gain?

Under any circumstances this should be considered criminal behavior. It used to be. If city officials were caught padding their own pockets or those of their friends it was considered graft. That's why RICO [Racketeer Influenced and Corrupt Organizations Act] laws were created.

Finally, five black robes [Supreme Court justices] named Stevens, Souter, Ginsburg, Kennedy, and Breyer shock the nation by ruling that officials who have behaved like Tony Soprano [fictional TV crime boss] are in the right and you have to vacate your property.

The Supreme Court Ruling Violated the Constitution

These four men and one woman have ruled that the United States Constitution is truly meaningless. Their ruling in the *Kelo* case declared that Americans own nothing. After declaring that all property is subject to the whim of a government official, it's just a short trip to declaring that government can now confiscate anything we own; anything we create; anything we believe.

Astonishing. The members of the Supreme Court have nothing to do but defend the Constitution and keep it the pure document the Founding Fathers created to recognize and protect the rights with which we were born. They sit in their lofty ivory tower, never worrying about job security with their life-time appointments. And yet, they have obviously missed finding a copy of the *Federalist Papers*, which were written by many of the Founders to explain to the American people how they envisioned the new government would work. They have missed the collected writings of James Madison, Thomas Jefferson, John Adams and George Washington just to mention a very few. It's obvious because otherwise, there is simply no way they could have reached this decision—unless implementing another agenda was their purpose.

I don't have the benefit of the Justices' grand staffs or unending salaries. But just a little research has turned up pretty much everything Stevens, Souter, Ginsburg, Kennedy, and

Breyer would have needed to reach a logical conclusion that protection of private property rights are the most important rights, vital to the very foundation of a free society.

Our Founding Fathers left no doubt in their writings, their deeds, or their governing documents as to where they stood on the vital importance of private property. John Locke, the man whom the Founders followed as they created this nation said, "Government has no other end than the preservation of property." John Adams said, "The moment the idea is admitted into society that property is not as sacred as the laws of God; and there is not a force of law and public justice to protect it, anarchy and tyranny commence."

One would be hard pressed to find a single word in the writings of the Founding Fathers to support the premise that it's okay to take private property for economic development. To the contrary, they believed that the root of economic prosperity is the protection of private property.

The Court Ignored the Constitution in Favor of Sustainable Development

So how did Stevens, Souter, Ginsburg, Kennedy, and Breyer miss such a rock solid foundation of American law? Perhaps they didn't. Perhaps they chose to ignore it in favor of another agenda. Specifically, Agenda 21.

For several years, certain members of the Supreme Court have been discussing the need to review international law and foreign court decisions to determine U.S. Supreme Court rulings. Justice Breyer has been the most outspoken for this policy, saying, "We face an increasing number of domestic legal questions that directly implicate foreign or international law."

What international laws are these? In general, the most pervasive are a series of UN [United Nations] international treaties, including several that address issues of climate, resource use, biological diversity, and community development.

Specifically, Agenda 21, signed by the United States at the UN's Earth Summit in 1992, calls for implementing what former Vice President Al Gore called a "wrenching transformation" of our nation, through a policy called Sustainable Development. Sustainable Development is the official policy of the United States and almost every single city and small burg in the nation.

Sustainable Development is top-down control, a ruling principle that affects nearly every aspect of our lives, including: the kind of homes we may live in; water policy that dictates the amount each American may use in a day; drastic reductions of energy use; the imposition of public transportation; even the number of inhabitants that may be allowed inside city borders. Most Americans have heard of a small part of this policy operating under the name Smart Growth. Agenda 21 outlines specific goals and a tight timetable for implementation. In June 2005, the UN held a major gathering in San Francisco where the mayors of cities from across the nation and around the world gathered to pledge to impose Sustainable polices.

In order to meet such goals, federal, state and local governments are scrambling to impose strict policies on development and land use. The use of Eminent Domain has become a favorite tool. Sustainable Development calls for partnerships between the public sector (your local government) and private businesses.

Now, as the public/private partnerships move to enforce Sustainable Development in local communities, an unholy alliance is also forming, allowing corrupt politicians to line their pockets and gain power as they partner with select businesses and developers to build personal wealth and power. They plot to take land that isn't theirs for personal gain, while claiming it's for the "public good." That's all the excuse they've needed to hide their true intent.

Americans Are Fighting Back to Protect Their Property

However, things have been changing as such brutal, organized theft has spread across the nation in the name of community development and environmental protections. Americans have started to fight back to protect their property. In Oregon, people went to the ballot box and shocked lawmakers by passing Measure 37, which says the government must either pay full price for any land taken, or waive the regulation and leave the property owner alone. In Wisconsin, the state legislature passed a bill to stop Smart Growth policies that are destroying property owners. In Michigan, the state Supreme Court overturned the precedent-setting ruling it made more than 20 years ago that allowed the use of Eminent Domain in taking property for private use. In fact, it was that original ruling that had been used by communities across the nation to justify their own Eminent Domain takings.

Clearly, the nation has started to rise up to stop this assault on private property. Without the power to grab property at will, the ability for communities to implement Sustainable Development has come into question.

Those who support Sustainable Development and Agenda 21 needed something big to put things back on track. The Supreme Court, which has already stated that it must look to international laws and treaties to decide American law, provided the answer. Stevens, Souter, Ginsburg, Kennedy, and Breyer chose Sustainable Development and Agenda 21 over the Constitution of the United States.

However, the effort may well be backfiring on the Sustainablists as the nation has reacted in force to protect property rights. Now, state legislatures and the U.S. Congress are rushing to produce legislation to restore property rights protections. Even Americans who have rarely uttered a political thought are suddenly becoming feverish with zeal for the Fifth Amendment. Americans may be learning all over again what the Founding Fathers knew—that the right to own and control private property is the most important right.

That is all well and good, of course, but Americans must do much more than just get upset. They need to get behind those legislative efforts at every level of government to assure passage. They must dig in at the local level to foil efforts by their mayors and city councils to impose Eminent Domain against their neighbors. We must run this organized theft (now masquerading as the "common good") out of town on a rail. And don't forget to leave room on that rail for Stevens, Souter, Ginsburg, Kennedy, and Breyer.

"The rumored death of private property rights is greatly exaggerated. The Kelo *decision does not expand the use or powers of eminent domain by states or municipalities."*

The Power to Take Private Property for Economic Development Benefits Cities

Eddie A. Perez

Eddie A. Perez is the mayor of Hartford, Connecticut. In the following viewpoint, he argues that eminent domain (the right of the government to take private property) is an important tool that helps cities create jobs, strengthen neighborhoods, and provide facilities and services to citizens. He declares that it is used sparingly and that the media have wrongly made people afraid that the Supreme Court's decision in Kelo et al. v. City of New London et al. *is a threat to homeownership. The ruling, he says, did not expand the government's power to take homes, nor did it condone the abuse of that power. In his opinion, if Congress were to pass legislation making it more difficult for state and local governments to take property, fewer people would be able to become homeowners. Moreover, those whose property has been taken in his own city have not only been well paid for it, but have often received government funding for their relocation.*

Eddie A. Perez, "Testimony of the Honorable Eddie A. Perez, Mayor, Representing the National League of Cities," U.S. Senate Committee on the Judiciary, September 20, 2005. Reproduced by permission of the author.

NLC [the National League of Cities] appreciates the opportunity to present a municipal perspective on the Supreme Court's decision in *Kelo v. City of New London*. Since the Court issued its decision last June [2005], the frenzied rhetoric and misinformation about the use of eminent domain for economic development purposes has been overwhelming and disappointing. To paraphrase Will Rogers, one of the early twentieth century's best political commentators, if all I knew about the *Kelo* decision was what I read in the newspapers, then even I would be worried that my hometown of Hartford [Connecticut] would bulldoze my house.

Once we get past the hype, two important points stand out. First, eminent domain is a powerful economic development tool used sparingly that helps cities create jobs, grow business and strengthen neighborhoods. No locally elected official whom I know would use eminent domain to undermine the integrity of or confidence in homeownership in his or her community. For urban America and communities of color, in particular, homeownership is the ticket to the American Dream. Second, if Congress were to pass legislation to hamstring state and local governments from using eminent domain, in some of our poorest communities I believe that we would have fewer people becoming homeowners, which means fewer participants in the Administration's concept of an "ownership society."

The Supreme Court's decision opened rather than settled the debate on the use of eminent domain for economic development purposes. It touched a raw nerve for most people about the boundaries between property rights of individuals and the authority of government. From the resulting fury, however, the Court's opinion creates opportunities like this morning's hearing for municipalities to contribute to a necessary national discussion about eminent domain.

The *Kelo* Decision Does Not Expand Municipal Power

The rumored death of private property rights is greatly exaggerated. The *Kelo* decision does not expand the use or powers of eminent domain by states or municipalities. Nor does the Court's decision overturn existing restrictions imposed at the state or local levels. The *Kelo* decision, as applied to the specific set of facts in New London [Connecticut], simply reaffirmed years of precedent that economic development is a "public use" under the Takings Clause. The Takings Clause, moreover, retains its constitutional requirement that property owners receive just compensation for their property.

Some legal scholars argue that the *Kelo* Court actually narrowed the eminent domain power. The majority opinion and concurrence by Justice [Anthony] Kennedy outline that eminent domain should only be exercised to implement a comprehensive plan for community redevelopment (1) based on wide public consultation and input, (2) that contains identifiable public benefits, (3) with reasonable promise of results that meet an evident public need, captured in a contract like a development agreement, and (4) with the approval of the highest political authority in the jurisdiction.

Hartford [Connecticut] has pursued a model of public development based on transparency, community consensus building, and true public benefit. As a result, we have used eminent domain as a last resort on six projects in the past 30 years. However, without the unambiguous authority to take land for a public purpose, the City would have had school, housing and development projects that cost hundreds of millions of dollars stalled or completed over budget.

The *Kelo* decision affirmed that eminent domain, a power derived from state law, is one best governed by the states and their political subdivisions. The *Kelo* Court affirmed federalism and the Tenth Amendment. Its opinion does not preclude "any State from placing further restrictions" on the exercise of eminent domain. Since the opinion's release, state after state—including Connecticut—have taken the Court at its word. Many state legislators have begun, or will begin during upcoming legislative sessions to examine their laws governing the use of eminent domain through proposed bills and study commissions. Regardless of the individual state outcomes, the Court correctly concluded that eminent domain is not a one-size-fits-all power, and that states are better suited than Congress to govern its use.

Hartford's use of eminent domain in the past has underscored the City's appreciation for those individuals affected so that the Hartford community can prosper. Frequently, these individuals are not only compensated for their property at prices well above market value, but receive significant and lengthy additional government funding for their relocation.

Recognizing that owner-occupied homes are more than just an investment for homeowners, I would advocate that governments that do not already do so explore ways to provide additional compensation to homeowners beyond "fair market" value where eminent domain is used for economic development.

Post-*Kelo* Caution with Eminent Domain Increases Among Cities

Cities, which generally use eminent domain as a last resort because of its significant cost in financial, political, and human terms, are now under an even brighter spotlight when it comes to the use of eminent domain.

In today's post-*Kelo* environment, there will be increased public pressure to prevent the use of eminent domain and more public scrutiny applied to municipal decisions to insure that its use occurs sparingly and only after exhausting all other options.

However, the availability of eminent domain to the City of Hartford has facilitated great economic and community growth. Projects such as Adriaen's Landing, a $500 million mixed-use development including a convention center, hotel, condominiums and retail, and The Learning Corridor, a $120 million, 16-acre complex of magnet schools developed by a nonprofit developer in one of Hartford's poorest neighborhoods, would not have been possible without the City having eminent domain available as a development tool. These projects are pillars in our efforts to revitalize the City. These projects have created thousands of construction and permanent jobs. They have attracted new business, increased home values, and sparked millions of dollars in new private investment ranging from first-time homebuyers to large financial services companies. Their effect on the Hartford economy and the overall quality of life for our citizens is tremendous.

In addition to the economic value that these two projects create, it is important to consider both the short and long-term social implications of having these facilities and services available to Hartford citizens and the region as a whole. As Hartford continues to grow and become one of New England's most vibrant cities, the need for attracting new businesses is larger now than ever. Adriaen's Landing and The Learning Corridor will help foster a growing desire of businesses throughout the region to locate their headquarters in Hartford. The social and educational benefits of these projects will also provide a continuously more educated and more attractive work force for businesses looking to relocate in the region. It is also important to consider the increase in potential homeownership gained through projects such as these. By creating economic growth, these development projects provide the City with the increased capital it needs to continue providing affordable homeownership opportunities for Hartford residents. The power of eminent domain helped bring these projects to life.

The *Kelo* decision did not condone eminent domain abuse. "There may be private transfers in which the risk of undetected impermissible favoritism of private parties is so acute that a presumption of invalidity is warranted under the Public Use Clause," wrote Justice Kennedy in his concurrence. Let me remind the Committee that neither the majority nor dissent in any court found that the City of New London engaged in any illegal or improper action involving eminent domain for economic development. The U.S. Supreme Court wrote "the trial judge and all members of the Supreme Court of Connecticut agreed that there was no evidence of an illegitimate purpose in this case ... promoting economic development is a traditional and long-accepted function of government."

There is a way for citizens that are particularly upset with the use of eminent domain to voice their discontent. Hartford residents vote policymakers into office. If there is a concern over a certain policy, the remedy for citizens is to make their opinions heard not only through civic involvement and awareness, but also through the ballot box.

The *Kelo* Decision Highlights the Natural Tension Public Officials Confront Between Individual Rights and Community Needs

The anxiety people feel about eminent domain is real. Historical examples of governmental abuse to construct the interstate highway system and for urban renewal make people suspicious about how governments intend to use eminent domain following the *Kelo* decision. This history imposes a duty on local officials to explain governmental use of eminent domain with greater sensitivity to its personal impact on individuals.

The press has incorrectly reported that the *Kelo* decision greatly expands local government authority giving city leaders permission to take homes without warning and without adequate compensation. This feeds the public's fears that bulldozers, which allegedly stand at Grandma's gate, engines roaring, are heading next for their homes.

A faulty distinction that places individual property rights in direct opposition to the use of eminent domain has emerged since the *Kelo* decision. Let me set the record straight with a brief review of the City of Hartford's commitment to homeownership. The City of Hartford has been at the forefront of the movement to increase homeownership in the State of Connecticut. Increasing the number of residents in Hartford who are able to own a home has been a cornerstone of my administration. I have a great concern for the City's homeowners whose opinions are of the utmost importance when discussing any development project in Hartford. The City has continued to take dramatic steps to provide millions of dollars each year to support citizens in their efforts to become homeowners. In the last year alone, the City of Hartford has spent over $5 million dollars on various initiatives to increase the homeownership rate, providing numerous Hartford residents with their first opportunity to own a home.

Additionally, the Neighborhoods of Hartford Initiative was developed to focus on the needs of each neighborhood and provide continuous support in helping each individual community address the issue of homeownership. From these initiatives and numerous others, there have been more than 1,000 new homeowners in the City of Hartford since 2001. Protecting and advocating for homeownership in Hartford is critical to help provide for the well-being of the Hartford community as a whole.

One of the most important responsibilities of any city government is to provide for the economic and cultural growth of the community while balancing the rights of the individuals that make up that community.

Eminent Domain Is Not Used for Private Benefit

Municipal officials know from experience what the judiciary has affirmed through precedent that economic development is a public use. By subjecting development projects to public debate and by planning these projects with the public welfare in mind, Hartford is able to use eminent domain prudently to allow the City and its citizens to develop the community in a way that is transparent and beneficial for all residents. The limited use of eminent domain for economic projects geared towards the well-being of the community will only increase the potential for more Hartford residents to realize their dream of owning a home.

Legislation that prohibits the use of eminent domain solely to provide for private gain is understandable. Property rights activists, however, cloud the issue for the public by linking the accepted legal principle that economic development is a public use with the inappropriate tactic of taking real property from A and giving it to B, for B's sole, private benefit. . . .

Municipal leaders have a responsibility to engage in public conversation about eminent domain that can help dispel inaccuracies and stereotypes.

Property rights activists, on the other hand, need to understand there is a delicate balance between minimizing the burdens on individuals and maximizing benefits to the community.

The art of compromise is essential going forward.

| "When an area is taken for 'economic development,' low-income families are driven out of their neighborhoods and find that they cannot afford to live in the 'revitalized' communities."

The Taking of Homeowners' Property for Economic Development Harms Minorities

Hilary O. Shelton

Hilary O. Shelton is the director of the Washington Bureau for the National Association for the Advancement of Colored People (NAACP). In the following viewpoint, he argues that eminent domain (the right of the government to take private property) is especially hard on African Americans and other racial minorities. In the first place, he says, it targets minority neighborhoods; many have been destroyed in the past by municipal projects aimed at economic redevelopment. He maintains that cities also choose to take areas with low property values because this costs the least. And when low-income families are forced to leave their homes, he argues, they find that they cannot afford to live in those neighborhoods after redevelopment has taken place. Shelton says that even the threat of a neighborhood being taken over by the government discourages residents from improving their communities, since they fear that their efforts will be wasted.

Hilary O. Shelton, testimony before the U.S. Senate Committee on the Judiciary, September 20, 2005. Reproduced by permission of the author.

138

Given our Nation's sorry history of racism, bigotry, and a basic disregard on the part of many elected officials to the concerns and rights of racial and ethnic minority Americans, it should come as no surprise that the NAACP [National Association for the Advancement of Colored People] was very disappointed by the *Kelo [v. City of New London* (2005)] decision. In fact, we were one of several groups to file an Amicus [Friend of the Court] Brief with the Supreme Court in support of the New London, Connecticut, homeowners.

Racial and ethnic minorities are not just affected more often by the exercise of eminent domain power, but they are almost always affected differently and more profoundly. The expansion of eminent domain to allow the government or its designee to take property simply by asserting that it can put the property to a higher use will systemically sanction transfers from those with less resources to those with more.

Eminent Domain Targets Minority Neighborhoods

The history of eminent domain is rife with abuse specifically targeting minority neighborhoods. Indeed, the displacement of African Americans and urban renewal projects are so intertwined that "urban renewal" was often referred to as "Black Removal." The vast disparities of African Americans or other racial or ethnic minorities that have been removed from their homes due to eminent domain actions are well documented.

A 2004 study estimated that 1,600 African American neighborhoods were destroyed by municipal projects in Los Angeles. In San Jose, California, 95 percent of the properties targeted for economic redevelopment are Hispanic or Asian-owned, despite the fact that only 30 percent of businesses in that area are owned by racial or ethnic minorities. In Mt. Holly Township, New Jersey, officials have targeted for economic redevelopment a neighborhood in which the percentage of African American residents, 44 percent, is twice that of the entire township and nearly triple that of Burlington County. Lastly, according to a 1989 study 90 percent of the 10,000 families displaced by highway projects in Baltimore [, Maryland] were African Americans.

The motives behind the disparities are varied. Many of the studies I mentioned in the previous paragraph contend that the goal of many of these displacements is to segregate and maintain the isolation of poor, minority, and otherwise outcast populations. Furthermore, condemnations in low-income or predominantly minority neighborhoods are often easier to accomplish because these groups are less likely, or often unable, to contest the action either politically or in the courts.

Lastly, municipalities often look for areas with low property values when deciding where to pursue redevelopment projects because it costs the condemning authority less and thus the state or local government gains more, financially, when they replace areas with low property values with those with higher values. Thus, even if you dismiss all other motivations, allowing municipalities to pursue eminent domain for private development as was upheld by the U.S. Supreme Court in *Kelo* will clearly have a disparate impact on African Americans and other racial and ethnic minorities.

Negative Impact of Takings on Minorities

As I said at the beginning of my testimony, not only are African Americans and other racial and ethnic minorities more likely to be subject to eminent domain, but the negative impact of these takings on these men, women and families is much greater.

First, the term "just compensation," when used in eminent domain cases, is almost always a misnomer. The fact that a particular property is identified and designated for "economic development" almost certainly means that the market is currently undervaluing that property or that the property has some "trapped" value that the market is not yet recognizing.

Moreover, when an area is taken for "economic development," low-income families are driven out of their neighborhoods and find that they cannot afford to live in the "revitalized" communities; the remaining "affordable" housing in the area is almost certain to become less so. When the goal is to increase the area's tax base, it only makes sense that the previous low-income residents will not be able to remain in the area. This is borne out not only by common sense, but also by statistics: one study for the mid-1980's showed that 86 percent of those relocated by an exercise of the eminent domain power were paying more rent at their new residences, with the median rent almost doubling.

Furthermore, to the extent that such exercise of the takings power is more likely to occur in areas with significant racial and ethnic minority populations, and even assuming a proper motive on the part of the government, the effect will likely be to upset organized minority communities. This dispersion both eliminates, or at the very least drastically undermines, established community support mechanisms and has a deleterious effect on those groups' ability to exercise that little political power they may have established. In fact, the very threat of such takings will also hinder the development of stronger ethnic and racial minority communities. The incentive to invest in one's community, financially and otherwise, directly correlates with confidence in one's ability to realize the fruits of such efforts. By broadening the permissible uses of eminent domain in a way that is not limited by specific criteria, many minority neighborhoods will be at increased risk of having property taken. Individuals in those areas will thus have even less incentive to engage in community-building for fear that such efforts will be wasted.

In conclusion, allow me to reiterate the concerns of the NAACP that the *Kelo* decision will prove to be especially harmful to African Americans and other racial and ethnic minority Americans. By allowing pure economic development motives to constitute public use for eminent domain purposes, state and local governments will now infringe on the property rights of those with less economic and political power with more regularity. And, as I have testified today, these groups, low-income Americans, and a disparate number of African Americans and other racial and ethnic minority Americans, are the least able to bear this burden.

"One of the most surprising claims about Kelo *is that it lowers the level of scrutiny that courts are to apply to public use determinations."*

Common Criticisms of the *Kelo* Decision Are Based on Myths

Thomas W. Merrill

Thomas W. Merrill is a law professor at Columbia Law School in New York. In the following viewpoint, he discusses five claims commonly made about the Supreme Court's ruling in Kelo et al. v. City of New London et al. *that he believes are myths. First, he says that it is untrue that* Kelo *was the first decision in which the Court authorized governments to take property for economic development. Second, it is untrue that the decision allows property to be taken just to create jobs or generate higher tax revenues. Third, Merrill explains that the ruling does not lower the standards courts must use when deciding whether property is being taken for a legitimate public use; rather, it raises them. Fourth, in his opinion the Court did not ignore the original meaning of the Fifth Amendment's takings clause, because its wording does not make clear what the Framers really meant. And fifth, he believes that the ruling is not a particular threat to minorities, because they would be targeted even more if takings were limited to blighted areas rather than being allowed for the purpose of creating positive benefits to communities.*

Thomas W. Merrill, testimony before the U.S. Senate Committee on the Judiciary, September 20, 2005. Reproduced by permission of the author.

Kelo v. City of New London, is unique in modern annals of law in terms of the negative response it has evoked. The initial reaction by lawyers familiar with the case was one of unsurprise. Within days, however, the decision began to gather widespread criticism in the media and among others less familiar with the process of eminent domain and the history of judicial decisions interpreting the "public use" requirement. Before undertaking far-reaching reforms of the eminent domain system that would seek to prohibit States and local governments from using eminent domain for economic development purposes, it is important to understand just what *Kelo* did and did not decide, and what may be significant about the decision. Accordingly, I will begin by addressing five myths about *Kelo* which I believe need to be dispelled.

Myth One: Kelo *breaks new ground by authorizing the use of eminent domain solely for economic development.*

Echoing Justice [Sandra Day] O'Connor's dissenting opinion, it is widely asserted that *Kelo* is the first decision in which the Supreme Court permitted the use of eminent domain solely for economic development. By giving its approval to this new use of eminent domain, it is asserted, the Court has provided a roadmap for an unprecedented—and frightening—expansion in the use of eminent domain.

The claim that economic development takings had never been previously upheld by the Court requires that one engage in considerable gymnastics with the relevant precedent. In particular, it requires that two propositions be established: (1) the universe of relevant precedent is limited to two decisions—*Berman v. Parker* [(1954)] and *Hawaii Housing Authority v. Midkiff* [(1984)]—and (2) those precedents are implicitly limited (it cannot be claimed that they are expressly so limited) to takings designed to overcome some "precondemnation use" that inflicts "affirmative harm on society."

As Justice [John Paul] Stevens patiently explained in his majority opinion, however, neither proposition is true. . . .

[He] concluded that "[p]romoting economic development is a traditional and long accepted function of government"—surely an irrefutable proposition—and that there was "no principled way" of distinguishing what the petitioners characterized as economic development "from the other public purposes that we have recognized."

Myth Two: Kelo *authorizes condemnations where the only justification is a change in use of the property that will create new jobs or generate higher tax revenues.*

The possibility that eminent domain could be justified solely on the ground that it would increase the assessed valuation of property was raised at the oral argument in *Kelo.* Justice O'Connor's dissenting opinion, which is based largely on a slippery slope argument, makes much of this possibility, building to her famous line—"Nothing is to prevent the State from replacing any Motel 6 with a Ritz-Carlton, any home with a shopping mall, or any farm with a factory."

The Court in *Kelo* did not have to decide whether an isolated taking to produce a marginal increase in jobs or tax revenues satisfies the public use requirement. The New London Redevelopment Project before the Court was designed to do much more than achieve an "upgrade" in the use of one tract of land. As Justice Stevens recounted, the project was also designed to generate a number of traditional public "uses": a renovated marina, a pedestrian riverwalk, the site for a new U.S. Coast Guard museum, and public parking facilities for the museum, an adjacent state park, and retail facilities. . . .

Myth Three: Kelo *dilutes the standard of review for determining whether a particular taking is for a public use.*

One of the most surprising claims about *Kelo* is that it lowers the level of scrutiny that courts are to apply to public use determinations. . . .

In truth . . . *Kelo* intimates that the Court in the future may impose a higher standard of review in public use cases than has prevailed before. Before *Kelo*, courts merely had to ask whether the use of eminent domain is "rationally related to a conceivable purpose." After *Kelo*, courts are instructed to investigate the factual circumstances to determine whether the invocation of a public purpose is a "mere pretext" to justify a transfer driven by "impermissible favoritism to private parties." In terms of the formulation of the standard of review, *Kelo* was a significant victory for property rights advocates, a development completely obscured by the widespread denunciation of the decision.

Myth Four: The original understanding of the Takings Clause limits the use of eminent domain to cases of government ownership or public access....

Unfortunately, other than the language of the Takings Clause itself ("nor shall private property be taken for public use without just compensation"), there is virtually no direct evidence about what the Framers understood by the words "for public use." The phrase modifies "taken," and thus clearly establishes that the Takings Clause is about a subset of takings—those for public use as opposed to other possible types of takings. But this narrowing language does not necessarily mean that the Clause imposes an affirmative requirement that a taking must be for a "public use." It is also possible that the Framers were simply describing the type of taking for which just compensation must be given—a taking of property by eminent domain as opposed to some other type of taking, such as a taking by tort or taxation....

Myth Five: Takings for economic development pose a particular threat to "discrete and insular minorities."...

Justice O'Connor's ... position is that "public purpose" takings are permissible, but only if the taking is designed to overcome some "precondemnation use" that inflicts "affirmative harm on society." Translated, this means that eminent domain can be used for economic development only if there is a finding the property is "blighted." Would requiring a determination of "blight" reduce the danger of poor and minority communities being targeted for economic development takings? The history of urban renewal projects in the post-World War II era—much of which proceeded under statutes requiring a blight determination—strongly suggests that poor and especially minority communities were disproportionately singled out for condemnation under these schemes. Making "blight" a precondition of economic development takings seems designed largely to reassure the middle class that its property will not be targeted for such projects, not to protect the very poorest communities.

More generally, economic development schemes limited to "blighted" property are backward looking. They ask whether the existing use of the property has fallen below some benchmark that the dominant community regards as "normal." In contrast, pure economic development statutes—such as the one in Connecticut—are forward looking. They focus on the prospective benefits the community might obtain from a transformation in the use of the property.

CHAPTER 4

Landowners Cannot Sue the Government for Harassing Them over Land

Case Overview

Charles Wilkie et al. v. Harvey Frank Robbins (2007)

Frank Robbins owned a large guest ranch in Wyoming. He grazed cattle on it, mainly for the purpose of conducting cattle drives in which the guests participated. Because the mountainous part of the ranch was an area with great natural beauty, the Bureau of Land Management (BLM) wanted an easement over a piece of the property (the right to use it) in order to maintain an access road for the public. In fact, it had been granted such an easement by the previous owner of the land, but the government had neglected to record that transaction legally, and so Robbins had acquired clear title to the property when he bought it. When BLM officials demanded that he give them the easement without being paid for it, he refused.

For six years after that, BLM agents kept trying to obtain the easement, but instead of offering to pay, they carried on a campaign of harassment and intimidation against Robbins in an attempt to get him to give in. They trespassed on his property. They made disparaging remarks about him to others. They charged him with permit violations and denied him the long-term permit he needed to plan guest cattle drives. When a dispute with a neighbor over cattle trespass arose, they provoked an altercation, encouraged the neighbor to call the sheriff, and boasted that they had found a way to put Robbins out of business. When this didn't work, they brought charges against him for minor violations, some of which were false. In the case of one criminal charge, he was acquitted by a jury that reportedly was appalled by the government's actions.

The attempt to ruin Robbins's business went on, and it very nearly succeeded, for the number of guests he was able to attract dropped dramatically. The BLM revoked his cattle grazing permit, forcing him to redirect his guest cattle drives through a mountain pass with unmarked property boundaries, and then tried to catch him trespassing on federal land. Agents followed the drives in trucks and videotaped the guests, sometimes in situations where common decency entitled them to privacy. Eventually agents even broke into his lodge.

Most of these actions were not illegal, and those that were, such as trespass, were not serious when considered individually. Therefore, Robbins could do nothing to stop them. Although in principle he could have sued the agents in state court, he could not have obtained a judgment against them on the basis of any single act, and there were no laws that covered harassment by a succession of acts that were legal in themselves. Finally, he filed suit in federal court on the grounds that his constitutional rights had been violated, arguing that the Fifth Amendment forbids government action calculated to acquire private property coercively and cost-free.

There is a legal precedent set by the case *Bivens v. Six Unknown Federal Narcotics Agents* in 1971 under which federal officials must pay damages to people whose constitutional rights they have abridged. Both the District Court and the Court of Appeals ruled that this could apply in Robbins's case. However, the Supreme Court disagreed. Officials are within their rights in trying to obtain land, it said, whereas in *Bivens*-type cases they have tried to do something they have no right to do, such as restricting free speech. In their negotiations with Robbins, said the Court, the agents merely engaged in "hard bargaining." While they offered no money for the easement, they did offer things of value, such as the right to use government land, in exchange for it. The Court majority decided that although the agents might have gone too far in their actions, to allow them to be sued on the basis of *Bivens*—or under the Racketeer Influenced and Corrupt Organizations Act (RICO), which Robbins also asserted was relevant—would be unwise because it would lead to many other suits and the fear of being sued might prevent governemt officials from doing their jobs.

Justice Ruth Bader Ginsburg was horrified by this decision, as were many property rights advocates after it was announced. "The constitutional guarantee of just compensation would be worthless if federal agents were permitted to harass and punish landowners who refuse to give up property without it," she wrote in her dissenting opinion. Several bloggers commented that the case might have even more impact than *Kelo et al. v. City of New London,* which two years earlier had aroused a storm of protest. However, it has received little attention from the public, perhaps because unlike *Kelo*, it did not present a threat to ordinary people's homes.

| "Unlike punishing someone for speaking out against the Government, trying to induce someone to grant an easement for public use is a perfectly legitimate purpose."

The Court's Decision: There Is No Law Under Which Landowners Can Sue the Government for Harassment

David Souter

David Souter became a justice of the Supreme Court in 1990. Although he was believed to be a conservative when appointed, he has often voted with the Court's liberal wing. The following is his majority opinion in Charles Wilkie et al. v. Harvey Frank Robbins, *which involved the owner of a ranch who was harassed by government agents in an attempt to make him give them rights to part of his land. In it, Justice Souter explains the Court's ruling that the landowner has no legal grounds for suing the agents because they were within their rights to use "hard bargaining" in the attempt to acquire the land, and their actions cannot be classed as extortion. To allow lawsuits based on violation of a landowner's constitutional rights would invite claims in every area involving legitimate government action related to property interests, he says, and the fear of being sued would hinder regulators whose job it is to obtain land for the govern-*

David Souter, majority opinion, *Charles Wilkie et al. v. Harvey Frank Robbins*, U.S. Supreme Court, June 25, 2007.

ment. If there is a problem with agents pushing too hard, he declares, any remedy should be determined through legislation rather than through the courts.

[P]laintiff-respondent Frank] Robbins has an administrative, and ultimately a judicial, process for vindicating virtually all of his complaints. He suffered no charges of wrongdoing on his own part without an opportunity to defend himself (and, in the case of the criminal charges, to recoup the consequent expense, though a judge found his claim wanting). And final agency action, as in canceling permits, for example, was open to administrative and judicial review, as the Court of Appeals realized.

This state of the law gives Robbins no intuitively meritorious case for recognizing a new constitutional cause of action, but neither does it plainly answer no to the question whether he should have it. Like the combination of public and private land ownership around the ranch, the forums of defense and redress open to Robbins are a patchwork, an assemblage of state and federal, administrative and judicial benches applying regulations, statutes and common law rules. . . .

This, then, is a case for . . . weighing reasons for and against the creation of a new cause of action, the way common law judges have always done. Here, the competing arguments boil down to one on a side: from Robbins, the inadequacy of discrete, incident-by-incident remedies; and from the Government and its employees, the difficulty of defining limits to legitimate zeal on the public's behalf in situations where hard bargaining is to be expected in the back-and-forth between public and private interests that the Government's employees engage in every day. . . .

When the incidents are examined one by one, Robbins's situation does not call for creating a constitutional cause of action for want of other means of vindication, so he is unlike the plaintiffs in cases recognizing freestanding claims. . . .

But Robbins's argument for a remedy that looks at the course of dealing as a whole, not simply as so many individual incidents, has the force of the metaphor Robbins invokes, "death by a thousand cuts." It is one thing to be threatened with the loss of grazing rights, or to be prosecuted, or to have one's lodge broken into, but something else to be subjected to this in combination over a period of six years, by a series of public officials bent on making life difficult. Agency appeals, lawsuits, and criminal defense take money, and endless battling depletes the spirit along with the purse. The whole here is greater than the sum of its parts.

The Government Agents Had a Right to Bargain

On the other side of the ledger there is a difficulty in defining a workable cause of action. Robbins describes the wrong here as retaliation for standing on his right as a property owner to keep the Government out (by refusing a free replacement for the right-of-way it had lost), and the mention of retaliation brings with it a tailwind of support from our longstanding recognition that the Government may not retaliate for exercising First Amendment speech rights.

But on closer look, the claim against the Bureau's employees fails to fit the prior retaliation cases. Those cases turn on an allegation of impermissible purpose and motivation; an employee who spoke out on matters of public concern and then was fired, for example, would need to "prove that the conduct at issue was constitutionally protected, and that it was a substantial or motivating factor in the termination" [*Board of Comm'rs, Wabaunsee Cty. v. Umbehr* (1996)]. In its defense, the Government may respond that the firing had nothing to do with the protected speech, or that "it would have taken the same action even in the absence of the protected conduct." In short, the outcome turns on "what for" questions: What was the Government's purpose in firing him and would he have been fired anyway? Questions like these have definite answers, and we have established methods for identifying the presence of an illicit reason (in competition with others), not only in retaliation cases but on claims of discrimination based on race or other characteristics.

But a *Bivens* [*v. Six Unknown Federal Narcotics Agents* (1971)] case [a case based on violation of constitutional rights] by Robbins could not be resolved merely by answering a "what for" question or two. All agree that the Bureau's employees intended to convince Robbins to grant an easement. But unlike punishing someone for speaking out against the Government, trying to induce someone to grant an easement for public use is a perfectly legitimate purpose: As a landowner, the Government may have, and in this instance does have, a valid interest in getting access to neighboring lands. The "what for" question thus has a ready answer in terms of lawful conduct.

Robbins's challenge, therefore, is not to the object the Government seeks to achieve, and for the most part his argument is not that the means the Government used were necessarily illegitimate; rather, he says that defendants simply demanded too much and went too far. But as soon as Robbins's claim is framed this way, the line-drawing difficulties it creates are immediately apparent. A "too much" kind of liability standard (if standard at all) can never be as reliable a guide to conduct and to any subsequent liability as a "what for" standard, and that reason counts against recognizing freestanding liability in a case like this.

The impossibility of fitting Robbins's claim into the simple "what for" framework is demonstrated, repeatedly, by recalling the various actions he complains about. Most of them, such as strictly enforcing rules against trespass or conditions on grazing permits, are legitimate tactics designed to improve the Government's negotiating position. Just as a private landowner, when frustrated at a neighbor's stubbornness in refusing an easement, may press charges of trespass every time a cow wanders across the property line or call the authorities to report every land-use violation, the Government too may stand firm on its rights and use its power to protect public property interests. Though Robbins protests that the Government was trying to extract the easement for free instead of negotiating, that line is slippery even in this case; the Government was not offering to buy the easement, but it did have valuable things to offer in exchange, like continued permission for Robbins to use Government land on favorable terms (at least to the degree that the terms of a permit were subject to discretion).

It is true that the Government is no ordinary landowner, with its immense economic power, its role as trustee for the public, its right to cater to particular segments of the public (like the recreational users who would take advantage of the right-of-way to get to remote tracts), and its wide discretion to bring enforcement actions. But in many ways, the Government deals with its neighbors as one owner among the rest (albeit a powerful one). Each may seek benefits from the others, and each may refuse to deal with the others by insisting on valuable consideration for anything in return. And as a potential contracting party, each neighbor is entitled to drive a hard bargain, as even Robbins acknowledges. That, after all, is what Robbins did by flatly refusing to regrant the easement without further recompense, and that is what the defendant employees did on behalf of the Government. So long as they had authority to withhold or withdraw permission to use Government land and to enforce the trespass and land-use rules (as the IBLA [Interior Board of Land Appeals] confirmed that they did have at least most of the time), they were within their rights to make it plain that Robbins's willingness to give the easement would determine how complaisant they would be about his trespasses on public land, when they had discretion to enforce the law to the letter.

Most of Robbins's Charges Concerned Actions That Were Legal

Robbins does make a few allegations, like the unauthorized survey and the unlawful entry into the lodge, that charge defendants with illegal action plainly going beyond hard bargaining. If those were the only coercive acts charged, Robbins could avoid the "too much" problem by fairly describing the Government behavior alleged as illegality in attempting to obtain a property interest for nothing, but that is not a fair summary of the body of allegations before us, according to which defendants' improper exercise of the Government's "regulatory powers" is essential to the claim. Rather, the bulk of Robbins's charges go to actions that, on their own, fall within the Government's enforcement power.

It would not answer the concerns just expressed to change conceptual gears and consider the more abstract concept of liability for retaliatory or undue pressure on a property owner for standing firm on property rights; looking at the claim that way would not eliminate the problem of degree, and it would raise a further reason to balk at recognizing a *Bivens* claim. For at this high level of generality, a *Bivens* action to redress retaliation against those who resist Government impositions on their property rights would invite claims in every sphere of legitimate governmental action affecting property interests, from negotiating tax claim settlements to enforcing Occupational Safety and Health Administration [OSHA] regulations. . . .

The point here is not to deny that Government employees sometimes overreach, for of course they do, and they may have done so here if all the allegations are true. The point is the reasonable fear that a general *Bivens* cure would be worse than the disease.

In sum, defendants were acting in the name of the Bureau, which had the authority to grant (and had given) Robbins some use of public lands under its control and wanted a right-of-way in return. Defendants bargained hard by capitalizing on their discretionary authority and Robbins's violations of various permit terms, though truculence was apparent on both sides. One of the defendants, at least, clearly crossed the line into impermissible conduct in breaking into Robbins's lodge, although it is not clear from the record that any other action by defendants was more serious than garden-variety trespass, and the Government has successfully defended every decision to eliminate Robbins's permission to use public lands in the ways he had previously enjoyed. Robbins had ready at hand a wide variety of administrative and judicial remedies to redress his injuries. The proposal, nonetheless, to create a new *Bivens* remedy to redress such injuries collectively on a theory of retaliation for exercising his property right to exclude, or on a general theory of unjustifiably burdening his rights as a property owner, raises a serious difficulty of devising a workable cause of action. A judicial standard to identify illegitimate pressure going beyond legitimately hard bargaining would be endlessly knotty to work out, and a general provision for tort-like liability when Government employees are unduly zealous in pressing a governmental interest affecting property would invite an onslaught of *Bivens* actions.

We think accordingly that any damages remedy for actions by Government employees who push too hard for the Government's benefit may come better, if at all, through legislation. "Congress is in a far better position than a court to evaluate the impact of a new species of litigation" against those who act on the public's behalf. And Congress can tailor any remedy to the problem perceived, thus lessening the risk of raising a tide of suits threatening legitimate initiative on the part of the Government's employees.

The Agents' Actions Cannot Be Called Extortion

Robbins's other claim is under RICO [Racketeer Influenced and Corrupt Organizations Act], which gives civil remedies to "[a]ny person injured in his business or property by reason of a violation of [this act," and] makes it a crime for "any person employed by or associated with any enterprise engaged in, or the activities of which affect, interstate or foreign commerce, to conduct or participate, directly or indirectly, in the conduct of such enterprise's affairs through a pattern of racketeering activity." RICO defines "racketeering activity" to include "any act which is indictable under" the Hobbs Act as well as "any act or threat involving . . . extortion . . . which is chargeable under State law and punishable by imprisonment for more than one year." The Hobbs Act, finally, criminalizes interference with interstate commerce by extortion, along with attempts or conspiracies, extortion being defined as "the obtaining of property from another, with his consent, induced by wrongful use of actual or threatened force, violence, or fear, or under color of official right."

Robbins charges defendants with violating the Hobbs Act by wrongfully trying to get the easement under color of official right, to which defendants reply with a call to dismiss the RICO claim for two independent reasons: the Hobbs Act does not apply when the National Government is the intended beneficiary of the allegedly extortionate acts; and a valid claim of entitlement to the disputed property is a complete defense against extortion. Because we agree with the first contention, we do not reach the second.

The Hobbs Act does not speak explicitly to efforts to obtain property for the Government rather than a private party, and that leaves defendants' contention to turn on the common law conception of "extortion," which we presume Congress meant to incorporate when it passed the Hobbs Act in 1946.

"At common law, extortion was a property offense committed by a public official who took any money or thing of value that was not due to him under the pretense that he was entitled to such property by virtue of his office" [*Scheidler v.*

National Organization of Women (2003)]. In short, "[e]xtortion by the public official was the rough equivalent of what we would now describe as 'taking a bribe.'" Thus, while Robbins is certainly correct that public officials were not immune from charges of extortion at common law, the crime of extortion focused on the harm of public corruption, by the sale of public favors for private gain, not on the harm caused by overzealous efforts to obtain property on behalf of the Government.

The importance of the line between public and private beneficiaries for common law and Hobbs Act extortion is confirmed by our own case law, which is completely barren of an example of extortion under color of official right undertaken for the sole benefit of the Government. More tellingly even, Robbins has cited no decision by any court, much less this one, from the entire 60-year period of the Hobbs Act that found extortion in efforts of Government employees to get property for the exclusive benefit of the Government. . . .

Robbins points to what we said in *United States v. Green*, (1956), that "extortion as defined in the [Hobbs Act] in no way depends upon having a direct benefit conferred on the person who obtains the property." He infers that Congress could not have meant to prohibit extortionate acts in the interest of private entities like unions, but ignore them when the intended beneficiary is the Government. But Congress could very well have meant just that; drawing a line between private and public beneficiaries prevents suits (not just recoveries) against public officers whose jobs are to obtain property owed to the Government. So, without some other indication from Congress, it is not reasonable to assume that the Hobbs Act (let alone RICO) was intended to expose all federal employees, whether in the Bureau of Land Management, the Internal Revenue Service, the Office of the Comptroller of the Currency (OCC), or any other agency, to extortion charges whenever they stretch in trying to enforce Government property claims. Robbins does not face up to the real problem when he says that requiring proof of a wrongful intent to extort would shield well-intentioned Government employees from liability. It is not just final judgments, but the fear of criminal charges or civil claims for treble damages that could well take the starch out of regulators who are supposed to bargain and press demands vigorously on behalf of the Government and the public. This is the reason we would want to see some text in the Hobbs Act before we could say that Congress meant to go beyond the common law preoccupation with official corruption, to embrace the expansive notion of extortion Robbins urges on us. . . .

Because neither *Bivens* nor RICO gives Robbins a cause of action, there is no reason to enquire further into the merits of his claim or the asserted defense of qualified immunity.

> "It is inconceivable that any reasonable official could have believed to be lawful the pernicious harassment Robbins alleges."

Dissenting Opinion: The Fifth Amendment Forbids Government Action Calculated to Acquire Private Property Coercively

Ruth Bader Ginsburg

Ruth Bader Ginsburg has been a justice of the Supreme Court since 1993, and is one of its most liberal members. The following is a portion of her dissenting opinion in Charles Wilkie et al. v. Harvey Frank Robbins, *in which she relates in detail the harassment to which Frank Robbins was subjected by federal agents when he refused to give them rights to a piece of his Wyoming ranch. She criticizes the Court's ruling in the case, saying that it was not true that the harassment was merely "hard bargaining" and that Robbins should have been allowed to sue the agents because they had violated his constitutional right not to give up property for public use if no payment was offered. She declares that it was wrong for the court to deny him the right to sue on the grounds that it might open the door to many other suits—which, she says, probably would not happen anyway. Furthermore, Justice Ginsburg says, the agents were not entitled to immunity from suit because they should have known that their actions were not permissible under the Constitution.*

Ruth Bader Ginsburg, dissenting opinion, *Charles Wilkie et al. v. Harvey Frank Robbins*, U.S. Supreme Court, June 25, 2007.

Bureau of Land Management (BLM) officials in Wyoming made a careless error. They failed to record an easement obtained for the United States along a stretch of land on the privately owned High Island Ranch. Plaintiff-respondent Frank Robbins purchased the ranch knowing nothing about the easement granted by the prior owner. Under Wyoming law, Robbins took title to the land free of the easement. BLM officials, realizing their mistake, demanded from Robbins an easement—for which they did not propose to pay—to replace the one they carelessly lost. Their demand, one of them told Robbins, was nonnegotiable. Robbins was directed to provide the easement, or else. When he declined to follow that instruction, the BLM officials mounted a seven-year campaign of relentless harassment and intimidation to force Robbins to give in. They refused to maintain the road providing access to the ranch, trespassed on Robbins' property, brought unfounded criminal charges against him, canceled his special recreational use permit and grazing privileges, interfered with his business operations, and invaded the privacy of his ranch guests on cattle drives.

Robbins commenced this lawsuit to end the incessant harassment and intimidation he endured. He asserted that the Fifth Amendment's Takings Clause forbids government action calculated to acquire private property coercively and cost-free. He further urged that federal officials dishonor their constitutional obligation when they act in retaliation for the property owner's resistance to an uncompensated taking. . . . The Court recognizes that the "remedy" to which the Government would confine Robbins—a discrete challenge to each offending action as it occurs—is inadequate. A remedy so limited would expose Robbins' business to "death by a thousand cuts." Nevertheless, the Court rejects his claim, for it fears the consequences. Allowing Robbins to pursue this suit, the Court maintains, would open the floodgates to a host of unworthy suits "in every sphere of legitimate governmental action affecting property interests."

But this is no ordinary case of "hard bargaining," or bureaucratic arrogance. Robbins charged "vindictive action" to extract property from him without paying a fair price. He complains of a course of conduct animated by an illegitimate desire to "get him." That factor is sufficient to minimize the Court's concern. Taking Robbins' allegations as true, as the Court must at this stage of the litigation, the case presents this question: Does the Fifth Amendment provide an effective check on federal officers who abuse their regulatory powers by harassing and punishing property owners who refuse to surrender their property to the United States without fair compensation? The answer should be a resounding "Yes."

Federal Agents Harassed Frank Robbins

The Court acknowledges that, at this stage of proceedings, the facts must be viewed in the light most favorable to Robbins. The full force of Robbins' complaint, however, is not quite captured in the Court's restrained account of his allegations. A more complete rendition of the saga that sparked this suit is in order.

Upon discovering that BLM had mistakenly allowed its easement across High Island Ranch to expire, BLM area manager Joseph Vessels contacted Robbins at his home in Alabama to demand that Robbins grant a new easement. Vessels was on shaky legal ground. A federal regulation authorized BLM to require a landowner seeking a right-of-way across Government land to grant reciprocal access to his own land. But Robbins never applied for a right-of-way across federal land (the prior owner did), and the Government cites no law or regulation commanding Robbins to grant a new easement to make up for BLM's neglect in losing the first one. Robbins was unwilling to capitulate to unilateral demands, but told Vessels he would negotiate with BLM when he moved to Wyoming. Vessels would have none of it: "This is what you're going to do," he told Robbins.

Edward Parodi, a range technician in the BLM office, testified that from the very beginning, agency employees referred
to Robbins as "the rich SOB from Alabama [who] got [the
Ranch]." Trouble started almost immediately. Shortly after
their first conversation, Vessels wrote Robbins to ask permission to survey his land, presumably to establish the contours
of the easement. Robbins refused, believing there was no need
for a survey until an agreement had been reached. Vessels
conducted the survey anyway, and chuckled when he told
Robbins of the trespass. At their first face-to-face meeting in
Wyoming, Robbins bridled at the one-sided deal BLM proposed. But Vessels was adamant: "The Federal Government
does not negotiate," he declared. Over time, Parodi reported,
Vessels' attitude towards Robbins changed from "professional"
to "hostile," and "just got worse and worse and worse."

Other BLM employees shared Vessels' animosity. In one
notable instance, Robbins alleged, BLM agent Gene Leone
provoked a violent encounter between Robbins and a neighboring landowner, LaVonne Pennoyer. Leone knew Robbins
was looking for a water source for his cattle, and he called
Pennoyer to warn her to be on the lookout. Robbins, unfamil-
iar with the territory and possibly misled by BLM, drove cattle
onto Pennoyer's land to water at a creek. Pennoyer showed up
in her truck, yelling, blowing the horn, and bumping cows.
Realizing that he was on Pennoyer's land, Robbins started to
push his cows out of her way, when Pennoyer revved her en-
gine and drove her truck straight into the horse Robbins was
riding. According to Parodi, after the dustup, Leone boasted,
"I think I finally got a way to get [Robbins'] permits and get
him out of business." Leone pressed the local sheriff to charge
Robbins for his conduct in the encounter with Pennoyer, but
the sheriff declined to do so.

Leone cited the Pennoyer incident as one ground, among
others, to suspend Robbins' special recreation use permit.
That permit allowed Robbins to lead ranch guests on cattle

drives, which were his primary source of revenue from the property. BLM aimed at the cattle drives in other ways too. Undermining the authenticity of the experience Robbins offered his guests, BLM employees followed along in trucks, videotaping participants. The Government suggests that this surveillance was a legitimate way to document instances when Robbins crossed onto federal land without permission. The suggestion, however, hardly explains why, on one occasion, BLM employees videotaped several female guests who were seeking privacy so they could relieve themselves.

As part of the campaign against Robbins, Parodi was instructed to "look closer" for trespass violations, to "investigate harder" and "if [he] could find anything, to find it." Parodi testified, in relation to the instructions he was given, that he did not have problems with Robbins: He never found a trespass violation he regarded as willful, and Robbins promptly addressed every concern Parodi raised.

The Court maintains that the BLM employees "were within their rights to make it plain that Robbins' willingness to give the easement would determine how complaisant they would be" about his infractions, but the record leaves doubt. Parodi testified that he was asked to "do things [he] wasn't authorized [to do]," and that Leone's projections about what BLM officers would do to Robbins exceeded "the appropriate mission of the BLM." About Vessels, Parodi said, "[i]t has been my experience that people given authority and not being held in check and not having solid convictions will run amuck and that [is] what I saw happening." Eventually, Parodi was moved to warn Robbins that, if he continued to defy BLM officials, "there would be war, a long war and [BLM] would outlast him and outspend him." Parodi found BLM's treatment of Robbins so disturbing that it became "the volcanic point" in his decision to retire. "It's one thing to go after somebody that is willfully busting the regulations and going out of their way to get something from the government," Parodi said, but he saw Robbins only "as a man standing up for his property rights."

The Harassment Campaign Ruined Robbins' Ranch Business

The story thus far told is merely illustrative of Robbins' allegations. The record is replete with accounts of trespasses to Robbins' property, vindictive cancellations of his rights to access federal land, and unjustified or selective enforcement actions. Indeed, BLM was not content with the arrows in its own quiver. Robbins charged that BLM officials sought to enlist other federal agencies in their efforts to harass him. In one troubling incident, a BLM employee, petitioner David Wallace, pressured a Bureau of Indian Affairs (BIA) manager to impound Robbins' cattle, asserting that he was "a bad character" and that "something need[ed] to be done with [him]." The manager rejected the request, observing that the BIA had no problems with Robbins.

Even more disconcerting, there was sufficient evidence, the District Court recognized, to support Robbins' allegation that BLM employees filed false criminal charges against him, claiming that he forcibly interfered with a federal officer. Federal prosecutors took up the cause, but Robbins was acquitted by a jury in less than thirty minutes. A news account reported that the jurors "were appalled at the actions of the government," one of them commenting that "Robbins could not have been railroaded any worse . . . if he worked for Union Pacific."

BLM's seven-year campaign of harassment had a devastating impact on Robbins' business. Robbins testified that in a typical summer, the High Island Ranch would accommodate 120 guests spread across six cattle drives. As a result of BLM's harassment, in 2003, Robbins was able to organize only one cattle drive with twenty-one guests. In addition, Robbins reports that he spent "hundreds of thousands of dollars in costs and attorney's fees" seeking to fend off BLM.

To put an end to the incessant harassment, Robbins filed this suit, alleging that the Fifth Amendment forbids government action calculated to acquire private property coercively and cost-free, and measures taken in retaliation for the owner's resistance to an uncompensated taking. Even assuming Robbins is correct about the Fifth Amendment, he may not proceed unless he has a right to sue. To ground his claim for relief, Robbins relies on [*Bivens v. Six Unknown Federal Narcotics Agents* (1971)] *Bivens*, [the precedent set by a case that allowed suits for violations of constitutional rights]. . . .

The Court Should Have Allowed Robbins to Sue for Damages

The Court has so far [in previous cases] adhered to *Bivens'* core holding: Absent congressional command or special factors counseling hesitation, "victims of a constitutional violation by a federal agent have a right to recover damages against the official in federal court despite the absence of any statute conferring such a right." . . .

As the Court recognizes, Robbins has no alternative remedy for the relentless torment he alleges. True, Robbins may have had discrete remedies for particular instances of harassment. But, in these circumstances, piecemeal litigation, the Court acknowledges, cannot forestall "death by a thousand cuts."

Despite the Court's awareness that Robbins lacks an effective alternative remedy, it nevertheless bars his suit. The Court finds, on the facts of this case, a special factor counseling hesitation quite unlike any we have recognized before. Allowing Robbins to seek damages for years of harassment, the Court says, "would invite an onslaught of *Bivens* actions," with plaintiffs pressing claims "in every sphere of legitimate governmental action affecting property interests."

The "floodgates" argument the Court today embraces has been rehearsed and rejected before. In [*Davis v.*] *Passman*, the Court of Appeals emphasized, as a reason counseling denial of a *Bivens* remedy, the danger of "deluging federal courts with [Fifth Amendment based employment discrimination] claims." This Court disagreed, turning to Justice [John Marshall] Harlan's concurring opinion in *Bivens* to explain why.

The only serious policy argument against recognizing a right of action for *Bivens*, Justice Harlan observed, was the risk of inundating courts with Fourth Amendment claims. He found the argument unsatisfactory:

> "[T]he question appears to be how Fourth Amendment interests rank on a scale of social values compared with, for example, the interests of stockholders defrauded by misleading proxies. Judicial resources, I am well aware, are increasingly scarce these days. Nonetheless, when we automatically close the courthouse door solely on this basis, we implicitly express a value judgment on the comparative importance of classes of legally protected interests."

In attributing heavy weight to the floodgates concern pressed in this case, the Court today veers away from Justice Harlan's sound counsel. . . .

The Court's assertion that the BLM officials acted with a "perfectly legitimate" objective, is a dubious characterization of the long campaign to "bury" Robbins. One may accept that, at the outset, the BLM agents were motivated simply by a desire to secure an easement. But after Robbins refused to cover for the officials' blunder, they resolved to drive him out of business. Even if we allowed that the BLM employees had a permissible objective throughout their harassment of Robbins, and also that they pursued their goal through "legitimate tactics," it would not follow that Robbins failed to state a retaliation claim amenable to judicial resolution.

Impermissible retaliation may well involve lawful action in service of legitimate objectives. . . . BLM officials may have had the authority to cancel Robbins' permits or penalize his trespasses, but they are not at liberty to do so selectively, in retaliation for his exercise of a constitutional right.

I therefore cannot join the Court in concluding that Robbins' allegations present questions more "knotty" than the mine-run of constitutional retaliation claims. Because "we have established methods for identifying the presence of an illicit reason ... in retaliation cases," Robbins' suit can be resolved in familiar fashion. A court need only ask whether Robbins engaged in constitutionally protected conduct (resisting the surrender of his property sans compensation), and if so, whether that was the reason BLM agents harassed him.

The Court's opinion is driven by the "fear" that a "*Bivens* cure" for the retaliation Robbins experienced may be "worse than the disease." This concern seems to me exaggerated. Robbins' suit is predicated upon the agents' vindictive motive, and the presence of this element in his claim minimizes the risk of making everyday bureaucratic overreaching fare for constitutional litigation.

Indeed, one could securely forecast that the flood the Court fears would not come to pass. ... If numerous *Bivens* claims would eventuate were courts to entertain claims like Robbins', then courts should already have encountered endeavors to mount Fifth Amendment Takings suits. ... But the Court of Appeals, the Solicitor General, and Robbins all agree that there are no reported cases on charges of retaliation by state officials against the exercise of Takings Clause rights. Harassment of the sort Robbins alleges, it seems, is exceedingly rare.

One can assume, *arguendo*, [for the sake of argument] that, as the Court projects, an unqualified judgment for Robbins could prompt "claims in every sphere of legitimate governmental action affecting property interests." Nevertheless, shutting the door to all plaintiffs, even those roughed up as badly as Robbins, is a measure too extreme. There are better ways to ensure that run-of-the-mill interactions between citizens and their Government do not turn into cases of constitutional right. . . .

Robbins' Constitutional Rights Were Violated

Because I conclude that Robbins has a right to sue under *Bivens*, I must briefly address the BLM employees' argument that they are entitled to qualified immunity. In resolving claims of official immunity on summary judgment, we ask two questions. First, "[t]aken in the light most favorable to the party asserting the injury, do the facts alleged show the officer's conduct violated a constitutional right?" [*Saucier v. Katz* (2001)]. And, if so, was that right clearly established, such that a reasonable officer would have known that his conduct was unlawful.

The Takings Clause instructs that no "private property [shall] be taken for public use, without just compensation." Robbins argues that this provision confers on him the right to insist upon compensation as a condition of the taking of his property. He is surely correct. Correlative to the right to be compensated for a taking is the right to refuse to submit to a taking where no compensation is in the offing. . . .

The Court has held that the Government may not unnecessarily penalize the exercise of constitutional rights. This principle has been applied, most notably, to protect the freedoms guaranteed by the First Amendment. But it has also been deployed to protect other constitutional guarantees, including the privilege against self-incrimination, and the right to travel. The principle should apply here too. The constitutional guarantee of just compensation would be worthless if federal agents were permitted to harass and punish landowners who refuse to give up property without it. The Fifth Amendment, therefore, must be read to forbid government action calculated to acquire private property coercively and cost-free, and measures taken in retaliation for the owner's resistance to uncompensated taking. Viewing the facts in the light most favorable to Robbins, BLM agents plainly violated his Fifth Amendment right to be free of such coercion.

The closest question in this case is whether the officials are nevertheless entitled to immunity because it is not clearly established that retaliation for the exercise of Fifth Amendment rights runs afoul of the Constitution. The "dispositive inquiry in determining whether a right is clearly established is whether it would be clear to a reasonable officer that his conduct was unlawful in the situation he confronted" (*Saucier*). As noted, all concede that there are no reported cases recognizing a Fifth Amendment right to be free from retaliation. However, it is inconceivable that any reasonable official could have believed to be lawful the pernicious harassment Robbins alleges. In the egregious circumstances of this case, the text of the Takings Clause and our retaliation jurisprudence provided the officers fair warning that their behavior impermissibly burdened a constitutional right.

Thirty-six years ago, the Court created the *Bivens* remedy. In doing so, it assured that federal officials would be subject to the same constraints as state officials in dealing with the fundamental rights of the people who dwell in this land. Today, the Court decides that elaboration of *Bivens* to cover Robbins' case should be left to Congress. . . . If Congress wishes to codify and further define the *Bivens* remedy, it may do so at anytime. Unless and until Congress acts, however, the Court should not shy away from the effort to ensure that bedrock constitutional rights do not become "merely precatory."

"Governmental employees must have discretion to perform their lawful job functions without the threat of ruinous personal litigation."

Allowing the Government to Be Sued by Landowners Would Affect the Performance of Officials

Amber H. Rovner et al.

Amber H. Rovner was the lead attorney representing the National Wildlife Federation, Public Lands Foundation, and Wyoming Wildlife Federation in their amici curiae (Friends of the Court) brief in the Charles Wilkie et al. v. Harvey Frank Robbins *case. These organizations were interested in the case because they are concerned with the responsible management of public lands, which they believed would be hindered if officials who tried to acquire private property for the government had to fear lawsuits. In the following viewpoint, she argues that if government employees could be sued for extortion even though their actions were lawful, they would become reluctant to carry out their duties. Extortion, she declares, should be defined solely by actions, not by the thoughts or motives that lead to them. In addition, she points out that if the Court rules that what happened in this case was extortion, then the precedent would apply to many other disputes between citizens and the government, such as relations between taxpayers and the Internal Revenue Service.*

Amber H. Rover et al., amici curiae brief of the National Wildlife Federation, Public Lands Foundation, and Wyoming Wildlife Federation, U.S. Supreme Court, *Charles Wilkie et al. v. Harvey Frank Robbins*, 2007.

Despite performing only lawful actions, the petitioners nevertheless face treble RICO damages [payment under the Racketeer Influenced and Corrupt Organizations Act] upon a bare allegation of a motive to extort. "By these claims, Mr. [Robbins] seeks to have a jury decide whether [petitioners'] facially lawful regulatory actions were the product of unlawful motive. . . . [S]uch judicial review of the actions of [the petitioners] . . . would be unprecedented" [*Sinclair v. Hawke* (2003)]. Governmental officials who diligently perform their jobs have never been, until *Robbins* [also known as *Charles Wilkie et al. v. Harvey Frank Robbins*], extortionists.

Even assuming that the court of appeals correctly determined that an otherwise lawful taking of property by a government official with an extortionate motive violates the Hobbs Act [a federal law that prohibits extortion affecting interstate commerce], the court of appeals erred in denying qualified immunity. Even when a plaintiff has properly alleged a violation of a constitutional right, a government official is entitled to qualified immunity unless the plaintiff can also show that the "law *clearly established* that the [official's] conduct was unlawful in the circumstances of the case" [*Saucier v. Katz* (2001)]. To be clearly established sufficient to justify a denial of qualified immunity, "[t]he contours of the right must be sufficiently clear that a reasonable official would understand that what he is doing violates that right" [*Anderson v. Creighton* (1987)].

What was clearly established prior to *Robbins* was that obtaining property only through an illegal action—an action involving violence, threats, fear, or receiving property not under an official right—is extortion. That is, until *Robbins*, no court recognized that extortion also applies to attempted takings of property by a government official whose actions were specifically authorized by statutes and regulations. Therefore, before *Robbins*, no reasonable governmental official informed of Hobbs Act case law would have ever imagined lawful actions taken pursuant to duly promulgated regulations could fall within the scope of the prohibition of the criminal Hobbs Act. To do so would sweep both lawful and unlawful actions— essentially every action a government official takes—within the ambit of the Hobbs Act. Indeed, pre-existing case law characterized such a result as "ludicrous on its face" (*Sinclair*).

In light of the pre-existing contours of Hobbs case law, qualified immunity should be afforded to petitioners. Simply put, there was no way reasonable government officials could have anticipated that their actions that were lawful pre-*Robbins* might suddenly become unlawful post-*Robbins*. . . .

Expanding the Definition of Extortion Will Hamper Officials' Ability to Do Their Jobs

Finally, expanding Hobbs extortion to include actions taken pursuant to lawful government authority will send shock waves through governmental agencies who routinely interact with the public. This remarkable and erroneous decision, if not overturned, will impact a wide array of government officials by severely hampering their ability to perform their jobs.

A governmental official exercises discretion in many, if not most, official decisions. The exercise of discretion, especially when a government official is negotiating property rights, creates a tense relationship between a property owner and a government official. This relationship is emotional and strained at best. Moreover, "judgments surrounding discretionary action almost inevitably are influenced by the decision maker's experiences, values and emotions" (*Harlow v. Fitzgerald* (1982)]. In light of this contentious environment, discovery into the motive of a decision maker may be boundless. "Inquiries of this kind can be peculiarly disruptive of effective government."

The court of appeals' holding will expose government regulators to potential personal liability under RICO [Racketeer Influenced and Corrupt Organizations Act] anytime that regulators' disputes with citizens involve property. These acrimonious property disputes are fertile grounds for alleging that the government official made a discretionary decision with a bad motive. And under *Robbins*, a mere allegation of "extortionate intent" will be sufficient to haul a government official into court to face racketeering charges. Given this reality, the *Robbins* decision could perversely condone a form of extortion claims to coerce governmental officials to take or refrain from engaging in lawful regulatory activities. And, in turn, the looming threat of personal liability will surely "dampen the ardor of all but the most resolute, or the most irresponsible [public officials], in the unflinching discharge of their duties" (*Harlow*). If left unchecked, the court of appeals' decision will chill federal employees' diligent performance of their regulatory duties. To prevent such a preposterous result, governmental employees must have discretion to perform their lawful job functions without the threat of ruinous personal litigation.

Extortion Should Hinge on Actions, Not Thoughts

Under the court of appeals' view, extortion may hinge on the thoughts, rather than the actions of a government official. Performing actions according to law will not protect a regulator from a RICO charge. Identical conduct may lead to different outcomes depending on the state of mind of the defendant. This uncertainty in identifying extortionate conduct will further impede a regulator from performing his or her lawful duties. Furthermore, a state of mind analysis is a subjective inquiry.... The Court should bury the nebulous subjective intent test in favor of an objective test that focuses on a government official's actions rather than thoughts.

A government official's qualified immunity defense seeks to strike a balance between a citizen's constitutional rights and a government official's ability to adequately perform his or her job. Qualified immunity responds to the "concern that the threat of *personal* monetary liability will introduce an unwarranted and unconscionable consideration into the decision making process, thus paralyzing the governing official" decisiveness and distorting his judgment on matters of public policy [*Owen v. City of Independence* (1980)]. . . .

The court of appeals equated a lawful attempt to obtain property while having an allegedly "extortionate intent" with unlawful taking of property under color of official right. By so doing, the court employed a test of clearly established law that bore "no relationship to the 'objective legal reasonableness' that is the touchstone of *Harlow*" (*Anderson*). Under *Robbins*, a plaintiff's RICO claim is sufficient if the plaintiff alleges that the official performed lawful duties with an extortionate motive. Because proof of motive is a fact-intensive subjective inquiry, creative plaintiffs could easily allege an extortionate motive sufficient to withstand summary judgment. And without the ability to dispose of such a case before trial, the government official facing a *Robbins* extortion charge thus has essentially lost his or her qualified immunity. . . .

These *Robbins* extortion actions will arise in many contexts. Cases involving an actual or attempted regulatory or physical taking of real property are prime candidates for contentious dealings leading to allegations of extortionate intent. But the potential swath of *Robbins* sweeps much wider. For example, since IRS [Internal Revenue Service] investigations typically involve monetary and other property disputes, a *Robbins* extortion action could be filed on behalf of a taxpayer against an IRS agent. . . .

And the possibilities do not stop there. Whenever a property right is at stake, RICO liability will become an issue. RICO liability may also be found in cases involving intellectual property infringement claims asserted against the government, social security cases, government seizure of property, welfare benefits cases, and denial of insurance claims, such as

Medicare and Medicaid. Each and every property dispute potentially could spawn a *Robbins* action.

> "If any private neighbor did engage in the sort of tactics engaged in here, Robbins would have a cause of action—probably several—for harassment, intimidation, and threats."

The Supreme Court Employs a Double Standard in Judging Individual and Government Conduct

Timothy Sandefur

Timothy Sandefur is a senior staff attorney at the Pacific Legal Foundation, a Sacramento-based public-interest law firm that litigates for property rights and limited government. He is the author of Cornerstone of Liberty: Property Rights in 21st Century America. *In the following viewpoint, he argues that the Supreme Court's ruling in* Charles Wilkie et al. v. Harvey Frank Robbins, *which stated that the government was merely bargaining when it harassed Robbins for not turning over his land, used a double standard as compared to what would have been decided if an individual or a private company had harassed him. The real reason for the decision, Sandefur says, was that because the government intimidates and abuses property owners very frequently, allowing them to sue would result in so many lawsuits that the courts would be overwhelmed. In Sandefur's opinion, the* Robbins *ruling has given the government almost unlimited*

Timothy Sandefur, "Robbins and Retaliation Against Property Owners," *Pacific Legal Foundation*, June 25, 2007. Reproduced by permission.

power to abuse land-use laws, and it may therefore prove to have an even worse effect on property rights than the decision in Kelo et al. v. City of New London et al..

Today's decision [June 25, 2007] in *Wilkie v. Robbins* [herein known as *Robbins*] is a terrible disappointment, and proof once again of the double standards that the Supreme Court applies to property owners as opposed to the government. It's little wonder that home and business owners across the nation believe that their property rights are treated—as the Court itself once put it—as a "poor relation" to other constitutional protections.

One of the important questions in the *Robbins* case was whether the Fifth Amendment protects a property owner from government retaliating against him when he refuses to give up his land to the government for free. Before Frank Robbins bought his land in Wyoming, the former property owner had executed a deed giving the government an easement over the property. But the government failed to record the deed before Robbins bought the property unaware of it. And that naturally meant that the deed was no longer valid. Rather than negotiating fairly with Robbins, however, the government began a vendetta against him, demanding that he give up his property for no money, and harassing him until he would do so. They bullied him, broke into his property, drove away his customers, threatened him, brought frivolous legal prosecutions against him, and generally made his life hell in the way that only government can do. He filed a lawsuit arguing that this violated his right to say "no" to the government—a right guaranteed by the Fifth Amendment's reference to private property rights.

But today, the Supreme Court held that Robbins could not recover because the government was simply engaged in hard-nosed "bargaining" with him, and that it had the authority to do so even where those tactics were particularly harsh.

You know how it is—your property has some minor infraction, perhaps, and a government agent decides to make things hard for you by coming down hard on you for it and every other minuscule violation of obscure rules, until you finally can't take it anymore. As Justices [Ruth Bader] Ginsburg and [John Paul] Stevens put it in their dissenting opinion today, the property owner suffers "death by a thousand cuts."

But Justice [David] Souter, who wrote the majority opinion, held that the property owner cannot defend himself in such cases, because the government was only "bargain[ing] hard." The government was acting "as one owner among the rest (albeit a powerful one)," and "[j]ust as a private landowner, when frustrated at a neighbor's stubbornness in refusing an easement, may press charges of trespass every time a cow wanders across the property line or call the authorities to report every land-use violation, the Government too may stand firm on its rights and use its power to protect public property interests."

Yet if any private neighbor did engage in the sort of tactics engaged in here, Robbins would have a cause of action—probably several—for harassment, intimidation, and threats. It's safe to say that if a big corporation—say, IBM or Microsoft or ADM—were harassing people in this way, Justice Souter would be far more sympathetic to the plaintiff who brought such charges. Yet because it is the government—supposedly acting in the public interest—Robbins is not allowed to sue.

Allowing Such Lawsuits Would Overwhelm the Courts

The real reason for Souter's conclusion is clear: because government intimidates and abuses property owners so often that allowing such lawsuits would overwhelm the courts; allowing an "action to redress retaliation against those who resist Government impositions on their property rights would invite claims in every sphere of legitimate governmental action affecting property interests, from negotiating tax claim settlements to enforcing Occupational Safety and Health Administration [OSHA] regulations." To allow citizens to sue government agents who are "unduly zealous in pressing a governmental interest affecting property [that is Souter's euphemism for stealing land from innocent American citizens] would invite an onslaught of [lawsuits]."

This argument is often used to bar American citizens from asserting their rights, and in other cases, Justice Souter is roundly against it. Just today, in fact, in the *Hein* [*v. Freedom From Religion Foundation, Inc.*] case, Justice Souter rejected the view that allowing taxpayers to sue government for spending its money to support religious institutions would open the door to too many lawsuits. There, in footnote 1 of his dissent, he wrote,

> If these claims are frivolous on the merits, I fail to see the harm in dismissing them for failure to state a claim instead of for lack of jurisdiction. To the degree that the claims are meritorious, fear that there will be many of them does not provide a compelling reason, much less a reason grounded in Article III, to keep them from being heard.

But when it comes to property rights, Souter is far less solicitous.

Another example of the double standard comes in Souter's rejection of what he calls "the 'too much' standard." That is, Souter says that *Robbins* "says that defendants simply demanded too much and went too far," and "[a] 'too much' kind of liability standard (if standard at all)" would be "endlessly knotty to work out."

And yet Justice Souter has shown no such concern when confronted with the infamous *Penn Central* [*Transportation Co. v. New York City* (1978)] standard—which is the rule that (supposedly) allows property owners to demand compensation from the government whenever its land-use regulations "go too far." For decades now, property owners have complained that this standard is unworkably vague and that it virtually always allows government to get away with terrible infringements on the rights of home and business owners. In fact, the Supreme Court has never compensated property owners under the *Penn Central* "goes too far" test. But Justice Souter has followed the vague *Penn Central* test repeatedly . . . because, of course, it allows courts an easy route to ignore the rights of property owners.

Federal Agents Have Unlimited Power to Harass Property Owners

The bottom line after the *Robbins* case is this: Federal agents have virtually unlimited power to abuse their otherwise legitimate powers to harass property owners in order to demand that they hand over their land to the government. Given what Judge Janice Rogers Brown once called "the pervasively regulatory state, [filled with] thousands of petty malum prohibitum 'crimes'—many too trivial even to be honestly labeled infractions [but which] are nevertheless public offenses for which a violator may be arrested," it will be extremely easy for officials to pester landowners by bringing prosecutions over every minor and insignificant infraction against the land use laws. After such constant petty annoyance, property owners may finally just give up their land to the government. In this way, *Robbins* may prove ultimately to be worse than *Kelo* [*et al. v. City of New London et al.*].

Ironically it was Justices Ginsburg and Stevens—who are no friends of property rights, usually—who saw through this ruse. In their dissent in *Robbins*, they wrote,

> Taking Robbins' allegations as true, as the Court must at this stage of the litigation, the case presents this question: Does the Fifth Amendment provide an effective check on federal officers who abuse their regulatory powers by harass-

ing and punishing property owners who refuse to surrender their property to the United States without fair compensation? The answer should be a resounding "Yes."

I am reminded at such times of [nineteenth-century abolitionist] Frederick Douglass' comments on the *Civil Rights Cases* [an 1883 decision that struck down the Civil Rights Act of 1875]: "O for a Supreme Court of the United States which shall be as true to the claims of humanity as the Supreme Court formerly was to the demands of slavery. . .! O consistency, thou art indeed a jewel!"

"*[The court] ensured that even indisputable violations of constitutional property rights will be compensated less adequately than violations of other individual rights.*"

The Supreme Court Treats Property Rights as Less Important than Other Constitutional Rights

Ilya Somin

Ilya Somin is an assistant professor at George Mason University School of Law and co-editor of the Supreme Court Economic Review. *In the following viewpoint, he argues that the Supreme Court gives property rights second-class status relative to other constitutional rights. A basic principle of constitutional law, he says, is that for every violation of a constitutional right there must be an adequate remedy, yet Frank Robbins was denied the right to seek damages (payment of money) that would have been granted if the government had violated another of his rights such as free speech—for example, if it had tried to stop him from criticizing land-use policy. The Court in* Charles Wilkie et al. v. Harvey Frank Robbins *stated that allowing him to sue would invite too many other lawsuits; but, Somin points out, adherence to the Constitution is supposed to override all other considerations, including those of cost, and in court decisions not involving property rights, it normally does.*

L ost in all the attention devoted to the Supreme Court's more high-profile end-of-term cases was an important property rights decision issued on June 25 [2007]: *Wilkie v. Robbins.*

This case reinforces the long-standing second-class status of property rights relative to other constitutional rights. Ironically, the only dissenters in *Wilkie*—Justices Ruth Bader Ginsburg and John Paul Stevens—are liberals generally considered unsympathetic to property owners.

Wyoming rancher Harvey [Frank] Robbins alleged that the Bureau of Land Management [BLM] launched an extensive campaign of harassment against him because he refused to grant the BLM an easement across his property without compensation. According to Robbins, government agents repeatedly trespassed on his property and harassed his customers. In one instance, they even allegedly tried to videotape female customers in the act of relieving themselves.

Under the Fifth Amendment, government coercion to force Robbins to give up the easement without payment is a clear violation of the takings clause, which prevents private property from being taken for public use without just compensation. The government cannot use harassment and intimidation to try to force citizens to give up their constitutional rights. Because the case was at the summary judgment stage, the Court had to assess all factual evidence in the light most favorable to Robbins. Nonetheless, the majority refused to allow Robbins to seek a damages remedy against the bureau.

Inadequate Remedies

This was not in and of itself especially troubling. There are other ways to prevent violations of constitutional rights. For example, the Court majority noted that Robbins could file tort suits against the BLM agents.

The problem is that the majority itself admitted that those other remedies were inadequate in this case. As the Court acknowledged:

"Robbins's argument for a [damages] remedy that looks at the course of dealing as a whole, not simply as so many individual incidents, has the force of the metaphor Robbins invokes, 'death by a thousand cuts.' It is one thing to be threatened with the loss of grazing rights, or to be prosecuted, or to have one's lodge broken into, but something else to be subjected to this in combination over a period of six years. . . . The whole here is greater than the sum of its parts."

Yet the Court still denied Robbins the right to seek damages. This undercuts one of the most basic principles of constitutional law: that for every violation of a constitutional right there must be an adequate remedy. The *Wilkie* majority ignored this rule because of its fear that allowing "action[s] for damages to redress retaliation against those who resist Government impositions on their property rights would invite claims in every sphere of legitimate governmental action affecting property interests, from negotiating tax claim settlements to enforcing Occupational Safety and Health Administration regulations."

Ginsburg devastated this argument in her dissent. As she pointed out, most other government regulations affecting property do not in fact have an impermissible retaliatory motive of the sort Robbins alleged. She also showed that the majority's parade of horribles has not occurred with state governments, despite the fact that damages remedies have long been available for unconstitutional retaliatory action against property rights by state officials.

Under current Supreme Court doctrine, furthermore, a regulation does not violate the takings clause merely because it "affect[s] property interests." To cause a taking, the government must physically occupy the property (as the BLM sought to do in this case) or eliminate virtually all the property's economic value through regulatory action. Most other regulations are not takings, even if they substantially impair property values.

Yet there is a still deeper flaw in the majority's reasoning. By its logic, citizens should be denied remedies for the violation of their constitutional rights any time setting up a cause of action for a remedy would burden the government too much. But the whole point of making the Constitution the supreme law of the land is to ensure that adherence to the Constitution trumps ordinary policy considerations, including considerations of cost.

The Court does not hesitate to follow this principle in most cases where other constitutional rights clash with real or imagined cost considerations. Federal courts routinely vindicate free speech rights and Fourth Amendment rights, among others, in cases where doing so imposes costs on the government. Unfortunately, they are unwilling to extend the same solicitude to property rights.

Unlawful Means

Justice David Souter's majority opinion claims that the key difference between this case and other instances of government retaliation for exercising a constitutional right is the motive for the government's action. "[U]nlike punishing someone for speaking out against the Government," Souter explained, "trying to induce someone to grant an easement for public use is a perfectly legitimate purpose."

The problem with this reasoning is that constitutional rights restrict not only the ends that government may pursue, but also the means that it can use to achieve them. In *Wilkie*, the government's desire to acquire an easement onto Robbins' property was not in and of itself unconstitutional. But the effort to achieve this purpose by forcing the owner to give up the easement without compensation was an unconstitutional means to an otherwise legitimate end.

To take up Souter's First Amendment analogy: It is perfectly legitimate for government officials to try to stimulate public support for their policies. It is not legitimate, however, for them to suppress opposing speech as a means to this end. If public officials punish anti-government speakers for their speech, Souter surely would not deny the victims a damages remedy simply because the government's ultimate purpose was "legitimate." Yet he fails to draw the obvious parallel conclusion for property rights. For that reason, his opinion helps relegate constitutional property rights to second-class status.

Souter further suggests that the government's actions were just an instance of "hard bargaining" to achieve a legitimate end. That is a strange way to describe a six-year campaign of illegal harassment he himself analogized to "death by a thousand cuts." If the BLM had used the same kind of "hard bargaining" to force Robbins to stop criticizing BLM policy, most justices in the *Wilkie* majority would not think of denying him an adequate remedy.

No Damages at All?

In contrast to the other five justices in the majority, Justices Antonin Scalia and Clarence Thomas would abolish constitutional damages remedies almost entirely, whether the rights violated by the government are property rights or not.

These two conservative justices categorically reject the principle—most clearly established in *Bivens v. Six Unknown Federal Agents* (1971)—that federal courts may sometimes order the government to pay damages to remedy the violation of a constitutional right. In a concurring opinion joined by Scalia, Thomas called *Bivens* "a relic" and urged the Court to confine its application as much as possible.

The Thomas-Scalia view has the virtue of treating property rights the same as other constitutional rights. Yet its shortcomings outweigh this one strength.

Perhaps the most fundamental duty of the federal courts is to overrule and remedy governmental violations of the Constitution. In some cases, an award of money damages is the only adequate remedy available, or even the only possible remedy of any kind. On other occasions, alternative remedies are available but are not sufficient to fully remedy the violation of the victim's rights. This was true in *Wilkie* itself, as the Court recognized.

In such situations, the courts have a duty to provide a remedy that fully compensates the victim for the violation of his constitutional rights. Any other approach is unjust to the victim and provides poor incentives for the government by allowing it to avoid bearing the full cost of its unconstitutional actions.

Thomas and Scalia may believe that judicial decisions that order a damages remedy somehow constitute judicial policy-making in a way that decisions mandating other kinds of remedies do not. Damage remedies are indeed sometimes unwise or inferior to available alternatives. Yet a damages remedy is not inherently more "activist" than alternatives such as injunctive relief or invalidation of a statute. In many cases, an injunction or invalidation of a statute will actually constrain the political branches more than damage payments do. The former options forbid government action outright, while the latter merely increases the cost of engaging in it.

Second-Class

In the short run, the main effect of *Wilkie* is to ensure that some property owners will not have adequate remedies for violations of their constitutional rights by federal government officials. This is a potentially serious problem in Western states such as Wyoming, where the federal government has extensive landholdings and disputes between federal agents and local property owners periodically lead to violations of constitutional rights.

More broadly, *Wilkie* reinforces the long-standing second-class status of constitutional property rights. In previous cases such as *Kelo et al. v. City of New London* (2005), the Court often defined the scope of property rights in a much more restrictive way than is usually applied to "noneconomic" rights such as freedom of speech and religion. In *Wilkie*, it ensured that even indisputable violations of constitutional property rights will be compensated less adequately than violations of other individual rights.

At the same time, as Thomas' concurrence implies, most of the arguments for denying damage remedies for property rights violations can also be used to justify their denial for violations of other individual rights. Those who are content with the Court's relegation of property rights to second-class status should realize that the same fate may befall other constitutional rights that they value more.

Organizations to Contact

The editors have compiled the following list of organizations concerned with the issues debated in this book. The descriptions are derived from materials provided by the organizations. All have publications or information available for interested readers. The list was compiled on the date of publication of the present volume; the information provided here may change. Be aware that many organizations take several weeks or longer to respond to inquiries, so allow as much time as possible.

American Land Rights Association (ALRA)
PO Box 400, Battle Ground, WA 98604
(360) 687-3087 • Fax: (360) 687-2973
E-mail: alra@pacifer.com
Web site: www.landuse.org

The American Land Rights Association (ALRA) is a national clearinghouse and support coalition encouraging family recreation, multiple-use, commodity production, and access to federally controlled and state lands. Its purpose is to oppose restrictive land use designations that damage local economies, schools and roads in rural America. Its Web site contains action alerts and information about pending legislation affecting land use.

American Planning Association (APA)
122 S. Michigan Avenue, Suite 1600, Chicago, IL 60603
(312) 431-9100
Web site: www.planning.org

American Planning Association (APA) is a nonprofit public interest and research organization committed to urban, suburban, regional, and rural planning. It believes eminent domain reform must be done in such a way as to avoid unintended consequences that threaten to hobble the ability of local citizens to improve their neighborhoods and quality of life. Its Web site has a section devoted to news and commentary on eminent domain legislation.

California Alliance to Protect Private Property Rights (CAPPPR)
1107 Ninth Street, Suite 720, Sacramento, CA   95814
(916) 444-8781 • Fax: (916) 444-8785
E-mail: activist@calpropertyrights.com
Web site: www.calpropertyrights.com

The California Alliance to Protect Private Property Rights (CAPPPR) is a coalition of family farmers, community and taxpayer advocates committed to exposing the dangers and abuses of eminent domain. Though it is focused on California issues, its Web site contains links to articles and publications of wider interest.

Castle Coalition
901 N. Glebe Road, Suite 900, Arlington, VA   22203
(703) 682-9320 • Fax: (703) 682-9321
E-mail: info@castlecoation.org
Web site: www.castlecoalition.org

The Castle Coalition is the Institute for Justice's nationwide grassroots property rights activism project. The Castle Coalition teaches home and small business owners how to protect themselves and stand up to the greedy governments and developers who seek to use eminent domain to take private property for their own gain. Its Web site offers a Survival Guide for homeowners whose property in threatened, plus a number of other downloadable publications.

Cato Institute
1000 Massachusetts Avenue NW
Washington, DC   20001-5403
(202) 842-0200 • Fax: (202) 842-3490
Web site: www.cato.org

The Cato Institute is a nonprofit public policy research foundation that seeks to broaden the parameters of public policy debate to allow consideration of the traditional American principles of limited government, individual liberty, free markets and peace. Its Web site contains many articles about property rights, among other topics, as well as Cato on Campus, an online resource created for students.

Coalition for Property Rights (CPR)

2878 South Osceola Avenue, Orlando, FL   32806
(407) 481-2289
E-mail: info@proprights.com
Web site: www.proprights.com

The Coalition for Property Rights (CPR) is a public policy, education and advocacy organization which was founded to give property owners and property rights a stronger voice. Its mission is to educate the public and elected officials of the importance of American property rights and to defend these rights from further erosion. Its Web site includes information and news items, focused primarily on Florida issues.

Foundation for Economic Freedom (FEE)

30 South Broadway, Irvington-on-Hudson, New York   10533
(800) 960-4333 • Fax: (914) 591-8910
Web site: www.fee.org

The Foundation for Economic Freedom (FEE), which is one of the oldest free-market organizations in the United States, is a nonprofit foundation that aims "to offer the most consistent case for the first principles of freedom: the sanctity of private property, individual liberty, the rule of law, the free market, and the moral superiority of individual choice and responsibility over coercion." The archives of its magazine, *The Freeman*, are available online and contain many articles about property rights.

Independence Institute Property Rights Project (PRP)

13952 Denver West Parkway, Suite 400, Golden, CO   80401

(303) 279-6536 • Fax: (303) 279-4176

Web site: www.propertyrightsproject.org

The Independence Institute is a nonpartisan, nonprofit public policy research organization dedicated to providing timely information to concerned citizens, government officials, and public opinion leaders. Its Property Rights Project serves as a community resource on land-use issues—including but not limited to—eminent domain abuse, zoning regulations, and historical designations. The Web site contains articles and news items.

Institute for Justice (IJ)

901 N. Glebe Road, Suite 900, Arlington, VA   22203

(703) 682-9320 • Fax: (703) 682-9321

E-mail: general@ie.org

Web site: www.ij.org

The Institute for Justice (IJ) is a libertarian public interest law firm that engages in litigation and advocacy both in the courts of law and in the court of public opinion on behalf of individuals whose most basic rights are denied by the government, including private property rights among others. Its Web site contains detailed information about the cases in which it has been involved.

Pacific Legal Foundation (PLF)

3900 Lennane Drive, Suite 200, Sacramento, CA   95834

(800) 847-7719 • Fax: (916) 419-7747

Web site: www.pacificlegal.org

The Pacific Legal Foundation (PLF) is a nonprofit public interest legal organization that fights for limited government, property rights, individual rights and a balanced approach to environmental protection. Its Web site contains extensive information about many court cases dealing with property rights, plus editorials and several blogs.

Property Rights Foundation of America (PRFA)
PO Box 75, Stony Creek, NY   12878
(518) 696-5748
Web site: http://prfamerica.org

The Property Rights Foundation of America (PRFA) is a national grassroots nonprofit organization dedicated to the right to own and use private property in all its fullness as guaranteed in the United States Constitution. It publishes the journal *Positions on Property*. Its Web site contains many articles and links to related organizations.

Reason Foundation
3415 S. Sepulveda Boulevard, Suite 400
Los Angeles, CA   90034
(310) 391-2245
Web site: www.reason.org/eminentdomain

The Reason Foundation is a nonprofit libertarian organization that produces respected public policy research on a variety of issues and publishes the monthly magazine *Reason*. Its Web site has a section on eminent domain and property rights containing many articles and several videos.

Tahoe Regional Planning Agency (TRPA)
PO Box 5310, Stateline, NV   89449
(775) 588-4547
E-mail: trpa@trpa.org
Web site: www.trpa.org

The Tahoe Regional Planning Agency (TRPA) works to protect Lake Tahoe for the benefit of current and future generations. Its Web site offers detailed information about the lake and the regulations with which homeowners must comply, as well as current news about its activities.

For Further Research

Books

Bruce Ackerman, *Private Property and the Constitution*. New Haven, CT: Yale University Press, 1977.

Terry L. Anderson and Laura E. Huggins, *Property Rights: A Practical Guide to Freedom and Prosperity*. Stanford, CA: Hoover Institution, 2003.

Tom Bethell, *The Noblest Triumph: Property and Prosperity Through the Ages*. New York: St. Martin's, 1999.

Don Corace, *Government Pirates: The Assault on Private Property Rights—and How We Can Fight It*. New York: HarperCollins, 2008.

James V. DeLong, *Property Matters: How Property Rights Are Under Assault and Why You Should Care*. New York: Free Press, 1997.

James W. Ely, *The Guardian of Every Other Right: A Constitutional History of Property Rights*. New York: Oxford University Press, 1997.

Richard A. Epstein, *Supreme Neglect: How to Revive Constitutional Protection for Private Property*. New York: Oxford University Press, 2008.

———, *Takings: Private Property and the Power of Eminent Domain*. Cambridge, MA: Harvard University Press, 2005.

Eric T. Freyfogle, *On Private Property: Finding Common Ground on the Ownership of Land*. Boston, MA: Beacon Press, 2007.

———, *The Land We Share: Private Property and the Common Good*. Washington, DC: Island Press, 2003.

Steven Greenhut, *Abuse of Power: How the Government Misuses Eminent Domain*. Santa Ana, CA: Seven Locks Press, 2004.

David Lucas, *Lucas vs. the Green Machine*. Alexander, NC: Alexander Books, 1995.

Carla T. Main, *Bulldozed: 'Kelo,' Eminent Domain and the American Lust for Land*. New York: Encounter Books, 2007.

Dwight H. Merriam and Mary Massaron Ross, eds., *Eminent Domain Use and Abuse:* Kelo *in Context*. Chicago, IL: American Bar Association 2007.

Jennifer Nedelsky, *Private Property and the Limits of American Constitutionalism: The Madisonian Framework and Its Legacy*. Chicago, IL: University of Chicago Press, 1994.

Richard Pipes, *Property and Freedom*. New York: Knopf, 2000.

Richard Pombo and Joseph Farah, *This Land Is Our Land: How to End the War on Private Property*. New York: St. Martins, 1996.

Timothy Sandefur, *Cornerstone of Liberty: Property Rights in 21st-Century America*. Washington, DC: Cato Institute, 2006.

Jason F. Shogren, ed., *Private Property and the Endangered Species Act: Saving Habitats, Protecting Homes*. Austin: University of Texas Press, 1998.

George Skouras, *Takings Law and the Supreme Court: Judicial Oversight of the Regulatory State's Acquisition, Use, and Control of Private Property*. New York: Peter Lang, 1998.

Periodicals

Cindy Anderson, "A House Divided," *Yankee*, January 2008.

John Berlau, "Bailing Out Kelo," *American Spectator*, July 25, 2008.

Tim Cavanaugh, "Property Seizures and the New London Tea Party," *Reason*, November 2005.

Ryan D'Agnostino, "How She Beat City Hall," *Money*, September 2006.

———, "Where the Streets Have No Name," *Money*, December 2005.

Cornelia Dean, "When a Shoreline Home May Be a Public Nuisance," *New York Times*, July 4, 1992.

Economist, "Hands Off Our Homes," August 20, 2005.

Richard A. Epstein, "Supreme Folly," *Wall Street Journal*, June 27, 2005.

Richard A. Epstein and Asher Hawkins, "The Taking of Port Chester," *Forbes*, March 24, 2008.

John Feinstein, "Hostile Takeover," *Golf Digest*, November 2006.

"Fight Them on the Beaches," *Economist*, February 29, 1992.

Steve Forbes, "Jettisoning Justices' Injustice," *Forbes*, December 12, 2005.

Ted Gest and Lisa J. Moore, "The Tide Turns for Property Owners," *U.S. News and World Report*, July 13, 1992.

Linda Greenhouse, "Justices Weaken Movement Backing Property Rights," *New York Times*, April 24, 2002.

J. Humbach, "Whose Land Is It, Anyway?" *Audubon*, May/June 1992.

Terrence P. Jeffrey, "Government Shall Steal," *Human Events*, July 4, 2005.

James C. Kozlowski, "Revitalization Condemns Homes," *Parks and Recreation*, February 2006.

———, "*Tahoe* Tests Takings Clause," *Parks and Recreation*, February 2003.

Joshua Kurlantzick, "Condemnation Nation," *Harper's*, October 2005.

Matt Labash, "Evicting David Souter," *Weekly Standard*, February 13, 2006.

Pam Lambert, Debbie Seaman, et al., "Battling to Save Her House," *People*, December 13, 2004.

Charles Lane, "Justices Affirm Property Seizures," *Washington Post*, June 24, 2005.

Jonathan V. Last, "The *Kelo* Backlash," *Weekly Standard*, August 21, 2006.

Edward J. Lépez and Sasha M. Totah, "*Kelo* and Its Discontents: The Worst (or Best?) Thing to Happen to Property Rights," *Independent Review*, Winter 2007.

Eugene Linden, "Demanding Payment for Good Behavior," *Time*, February 3, 1992.

Lora Lucero and Jeffrey Soule, "A Win for Lake Tahoe," *Planning*, June 2002.

Timothy Lynch, "Tortuous Journey to Justice," *Regulation*, Spring 1998. www.cato.org.

Carla T. Main, "How Eminent Domain Ran Amok," *Policy Review*, October/November 2005.

———, "The 'Blight' Excuse," *Wall Street Journal*, June 23, 2007.

Robert Marquand, "Court Weighs Widow's Right to a Lake Tahoe View," *Christian Science Monitor*, February 27, 1997.

Avi Salzman, "Only 2 Holdouts Left in Eminent Domain Case," *New York Times*, June 11, 2006.

Avi Salzman and Laura Mansnerus, "For Homeowners, Frustration and Anger at Court's Ruling," *New York Times*, June 24, 2005.

Timothy Sandefur, "*Kelo*: Hope for Property Rights," *Liberty*, September 2005.

Phyllis Schlafly, "Conservatives Beating Back Court Attack on Private Property," *Human Events*, October 9, 2006.

Darrell Smith, "Uproar Over Property Rights," *Farm Journal*, November 2005.

Ilya Somin, "The Limits of Anti-*Kelo* Legislation," *Reason*, August/September 2007.

Mary Zeiss Stange, "Life, Liberty, and Property Rights," *USA Today*, November 2, 2006.

John Tierney, "Supreme Home Makeover," *New York Times*, March 14, 2006.

William Yardley, "After Eminent Domain Victory, Disputed Project Goes Nowhere," *New York Times*, November 21, 2005.

Index